$1.00

THE
MISSING LINKS
Golf and the Mind

THE MISSING LINKS
Golf and the Mind
by David C. Morley, M.D.

Technical Editor: Ken Bowden

tempo
books

GROSSET & DUNLAP
A FILMWAYS COMPANY
Publishers • New York

Copyright © 1976 David C. Morley
All rights reserved
ISBN: 0-448-14623-1
Library of Congress Catalog Card
Number: 75-13500
First paperback edition
Published by arrangement with
Atheneum Publishers
Tempo Books is registered in the
U.S. Patent Office
Published simultaneously in Canada
Printed in the United States of America

To Marion

Acknowledgments

WRITING A BOOK is a solitary experience, but no book is ever written without the contributions of other people.

I would like especially to acknowledge the great part Ken Bowden played in this whole experience. It was from his creative mind that the idea first came of investigating the mysterious role of the mind in golf. It was through him, as then Editorial Director of *Golf Digest* magazine, that I got my first writing assignment. It was because of his persuasion that I began this book. His editorial contribution in planning and shaping the work has been monumental.

I would also like to thank the great teaching professional, John Jacobs, for taking time out of his busy London life to talk to me about this fascinating subject over a steaming pot of tea.

I would not forget my dear friend, Russ Esty, through whose generosity I was privileged to play and become acquainted with the trio of golfing greats— Jack Nicklaus, Arnold Palmer and Gary Player.

Acknowledgments

In addition, I want to thank the brilliant playwright, Bill Brown, from whose nimble mind came, quite spontaneously, the title, *The Missing Links*.

Last, but not least, many thanks to my friend of long standing, artist Stan Drake, who got me involved in this wonderful world of writing in the first place.

Contents

Contents

Contents

THE
MISSING LINKS
Golf and the Mind

I

Why Golf Is So Different—
and So Difficult

GOLF is a game that is uniquely different from other games men play. For one thing, it doesn't require any exceptional physical gifts. To play golf well you don't have to weigh over 200 pounds, or stand closer to seven feet than six, or be capable of covering 100 yards in less than ten seconds. Nor is the game particularly demanding intellectually. To win the U.S. Open you certainly don't need the kind of brain it would take to win a Ph.D. in nuclear physics. In fact, if the example of quite a number of past champions is anything to go by, you don't even need to have finished high school to become a master of the links.

In short, golf seems to demand few if any of the attributes that are essential to achieve excellence in other games. And yet, as everyone knows who has tried it, golf is incredibly difficult to play well.

Why?

Some of the reasons are certainly physical, in the sense that repeatedly striking a golf ball hard and true

takes a lot of dexterity. Some of the reasons are certainly intellectual, in the sense that intelligence is
necessary in order to meet the game's strategical and
tactical demands. But there is more to it than that, as
the champions acknowledge when they so frequently
and insistently state that "Golf is 70 (or 80 or 90)
percent a *mental* game."

The champions are right, even though they rarely
try to explain exactly what they mean. There *are*
mental dimensions to golf that either are not present
at all or are of comparatively minor influence in other
games. That these mental factors are rarely publicly
discussed, let alone endlessly dissected and analyzed
like the physical elements of golf, is probably due to
their complexity and to their highly emotional (and
therefore intimate) character. And yet, as we shall see
as we look quickly at the most important of them, there
can be no doubt that they contribute enormously to the
difficulty of golf.

LISTENING TO TWO TUNES AT ONCE

ALTHOUGH golf is a game played with other
people, it is essentially an individualistic, and therefore a lonely, experience. The presence and demeanor
of the other people involved generally inject a spirit
of camaraderie into the game. But, at root, this overt
show of fellowship is a disguise masking an inherent
loneliness of endeavor often so intense as to be almost
existential.

Mentally, the golfer is almost always in the position
of listening to two orchestras playing two tunes at
once. Part of his mind is engaged in the light, warm

comradeship of like-minded people taking pleasure in the fresh air, the sunshine, the beautiful scenery, and so on. This part of his mind is bright and cheerful, bathed in the pleasure of that very enjoyable human experience.

At the same time, another part of the golfer's mind is deeply involved in a constant internal monologue involving his actual *performance* of the game. This part of the mind, separated from the other, is inward-looking, brooding, scheming, often worrying—in short, intensely concerned with the personal business at hand. Thus preoccupied, it wants to have very little to do with external factors—doesn't really give a darn about the balmy weather, or the lovely scenery, or being sociable. It is involved in a very private activity, in which there is little room for anyone or anything else.

This inner monologue is a very intimate process, and most golfers—even the best—try hard to conceal both its presence and its intensity. Many try to do so by appearing nonchalant, or at least fairly light-hearted, even when under the most intense competitive pressure.

The compensatory behavior of Lee Trevino, whose approach to the game sometimes seems to be casual almost to the point of frivolity, is perhaps the supreme example of this type of reaction to the threats of the internal monologue. Most of the time Trevino's ebullient facade very effectively masks that dark, somber side of his mind that is totally egocentric and antisocial, and therefore must be kept carefully hidden from the exterior world. It is when the inner monologue becomes so strident that it overpowers the facade that the exterior world sometimes glimpses another Trevino—the Trevino grumpily hurrying straight from the 18th green to the private haven of his motel room.

At the opposite end of the scale, a golfer will react to the inner struggle by almost completely excluding himself from the external world, even when operating within it. Ben Hogan reacted thusly, as did Jack Nicklaus in his early days. Hogan, and to a lesser degree Nicklaus, simply drew down the blind on that part of their experience beyond the internal dialogue. As a result, both often came across to audiences as antisocial, brooding, machine-like, and generally unappealing beyond their sheer golfing genius.

Hogan was thought of as a heartless machine programmed for victory at any cost, and ever ready to slam the door in the face of anyone wishing to examine more than his golf scores. Nicklaus's nickname, the Golden Bear, stuck with him not so much, in my view, because of his golden locks, but because he came across as an angry bear who glowered through the bars of his cage at anyone who dared interfere with his intense inner involvement. As he matured and met more and more of his goals, the internal dialogue became easier for him to handle, and he became a warmer, friendlier, more sociable being, increasingly aware of, and responsive to, the crowd and the drama of the spectacle in which he was so often a major actor.

This dichotomy within the mind is something that every golfer has to recognize and deal with. And it is one of the mental peculiarities that make golf such a unique—and difficult—game.

YOU'RE ON YOUR OWN

IN almost all games you play with other people, the actions of your fellow participants are much more than social functions. What they do dramatically affects what you do: the pitcher's moves in baseball determine the behavior of the batter; the action of the man who serves the ball in tennis determines the response of the person waiting on the other side of the net; and so on. But in golf all of the meaningful physical activity is strictly between the golfer and the ball. Even when he is playing a so-called "head-to-head" match, only through what he does with the ball can the golfer influence the play of his opponent. And when the golfer is involved with the ball, he must turn off all other functions of his personality. For these few moments he must shut himself off completely from the rest of the world and become totally preoccupied with the ball and its position on the golf course relative to the hole. What he actually does to that ball depends solely upon his own capabilities. He has no coach, no one to run interference for him, no teammates to help him. All decisions and actions are his sole responsibility.

However, once he has made his physical commitment and struck the ball, the golfer is free to relax and enjoy the company of his companions—and he makes a big mistake if he doesn't do so.

Most great golfers recognize the intervals between shots as periods of relief, when they can clear their minds of tension and other distracting influences, allowing them to recover from the intensity of that brief but lonely experience over the ball. Of course, no golfer can be totally free of some subconscious thoughts concerning the tactics of his game. But, if he is wise, in the intervals of relief between his shots he will turn *off* that internal monologue with as much deliberation as he turns it *on* when he addresses the ball.

Unfortunately, achieving this flexibility demands a

mental discipline difficult for most golfers to attain. Some seem to fear losing touch with that seething inner monologue, and their excursions into the social side of the game are thus at best tentative. They appear grumpy, moody, antisocial, giving the impression that the intervals between shots are wasted time. They would do better to utilize these respites by recognizing that the ability to tune in one world and tune out another actually increases the intensity of their mental concentration when they most need it.

THE EMOTIONAL IMPACT OF OPPONENTS

MOST golfers fail to recognize that golf is, in the final analysis, essentially a game played between the golfer and the golf course. Certainly, if more would grasp this, they would avoid a lot of mental pitfalls. However, although this is the *basic* truth, on a more obvious level the golfer is also competing directly against other people and thus is naturally interested in their games to some degree. The risk here is of emotional involvement *in*, rather than detached awareness *of*, the opponents' games. Many golfers, even at the pro tournament level, have discovered that their own games can be adversely affected by emotional reactions to their opponents' play.

This happens because in golf a participant is not only a performer, but by necessity a spectator as well. And the way the golfer handles this second role can affect the efficiency of his own game as much as the way he holds the club in his hands.

When the first player to tee off hits a booming drive

down the center of the fairway, the golfers who follow react in various ways. Many are threatened by such demonstrations of strength. They respond to the challenge by wanting to outdrive the man who has just struck the ball. Thus they immediately regress to the caveman situation of one man proving his superiority to another by some demonstration of brute strength. Their reaction is to swing the club with all the finesse of a Stone Age man smashing a club at a dinosaur. The result is almost always disastrous.

Other golfers allow themselves to be overawed by their opponents' demonstrations of strength. Their minds flood with negative thoughts, their muscles turn to jelly, their knees become weak, and their nerves begin to jangle. As a result, when they step to center stage, they are so filled with doubts that their efforts become just as ineffective as those of the golfer who turns into a gorilla any time he is threatened by superior strength.

Although these two reactions are diametrically opposite, the results are essentially the same: both golfers are victims of internal reactions to something that they have *seen*. In short, their emotional reaction to another's performance has devastating effects on their own game.

Objectivity in spectatorship is therefore another unique difficulty of golf. It is not easy to achieve, but it must be striven for. The successful golfer must not allow himself to identify *emotionally* with the actions of other performers, and the easiest way for him to avoid doing so is to recognize that these actions cannot in any way directly influence his own game. Emotional involvement with sporting performance should be reserved for the stadium or the TV set. It's fine to identify

with Joe Namath as you watch him complete a fifty-
yard pass, because you're not expected to get up from
the bleachers, or your easy chair, and do the same
thing. However, when you see a man hit a long ball
from the tee, and you're up next, you have to follow
him onto that same stage and try to emulate him. Any
time you let your emotions rule how you do so, you're
in trouble.

The better pro tournament players solve this problem by watching their rivals with a detachment that
allows them to derive, from what they see, certain
specific physical information that can be helpful to
their own games. For example, they look for such
information as the effect of the wind upon the flight
of the ball; the distance the ball rolls or kicks to left
or right on landing; the speed of the green as revealed
by the action of an opponent's ball; and so on.

The trick is never to get into the habit of making
judgments about your own game by comparing it with
other people's. That kind of emotional approach courts
disaster by opening the mind to all kinds of negative
feedback.

THE INFLUENCE OF THE BALL

GOLF is a ball game, of course, but what makes
it different from almost every other ball game is that the
ball doesn't move until the golfer hits it. This static
state of the ball encourages the mind to become passively related to it. In other words, the ball influences
the golfer's mind instead of the golfer's mind influenc-
ing the ball.

Staring at a motionless object does not stimulate the mind or the body into action. Rather, it invites immobility. For example, when a person stares at a crystal ball, his mind has a tendency to enter into the early stages of hypnosis, in which condition it becomes very open to suggestion—particularly to the kind of negative feedback mentioned a moment ago. The tendency for the mind to slip into a state of passive suggestibility, as a result of being "hypnotized" by the immobile ball, is thus another characteristic contributing to golf's unique difficulty.

To be successful as a player, the golfer must at all times relate to the ball actively rather than passively. *He*, not the ball, must be in control. Once the ball takes over, the mind becomes susceptible to myriad influences that can at best inhibit and at worst totally destroy the mechanics of swinging the club. We will look further into this problem in a later chapter.

THE INFLUENCE OF THE CLUB

NOTHING in golf is more unique than the strangely shaped implements with which the player propels the ball. The novelist John Updike referred to the golf club as a "silver wand, curiously warped at one end." Few people have given much thought to the mental effect of this oddly shaped instrument on the player. In most other ball-striking games the hitting surface of the bat or racket extends in a straight line from the shaft. This makes it much easier for the mind and body to execute coordinated movements, because the implement seems like a natural extension of the arm.

The fact that the hitting surface of the golf club is not in the same geometric plane as the shaft can subtly undermine the golfer's belief that it can actually do the job for which it is supposedly designed. The insecurity associated with such a thought is bound to create an appreciable amount of tension, which floods the golfer's nervous system and does all kinds of strange things to the tempo of his swing.

Then there is the factor that the shaft of a golf club is much longer than, for example, the shaft of a tennis racket, or even a baseball bat. Thus the ball is much farther away from the hands in golf than in baseball or tennis, and this factor is accentuated by the tiny size of the ball and the striking surface of the club. Again, more insecurity, and more tension.

YOU MUST BE YOUR OWN REFEREE

GOLF is a game played without a referee. In major tournaments there are sometimes official observers, but they remain quietly in the background. Yet no game has more complex or rigid rules and codes of behavior, and the responsibility for the implementation of those rules and codes lies squarely upon the shoulders of the individual golfer. He must be his own prosecutor as well as his own advocate. He must operate on the honor system. He is expected to know the rules and to abide by them.

This kind of situation simply does not exist in other games where officials are prominent and active. If a football player clips another player, the referee blows his whistle and calls a penalty. Because there are no such external judgments on the links, it is tempting for the golfer to break the rules: to forget a stroke, especially if he has made a lot of them; to nudge a ball that's in a bad lie when nobody's looking; to look for a lost ball beyond the five-minute time limit.

The golfer's powers for self-rationalization in situations like this are endless, which is why more liberties are taken in golf than in any other mass-participant game. The need for scrupulous honesty, and the guilt feelings that accompany rule-breaking, are yet further pressures adding to the difficulty of the game.

FEAR AND ANGER

GOLF certainly is a mental game, as all the great players agree, but it is not really an *intellectual* game like, for example, chess. No complicated mental gymnastics are required, nor is there any demand in golf for quick or spontaneous thinking as in games like baseball or tennis. The golf ball isn't going to take a bad bounce before you hit it.

In a curious way, the mental aspect of the game is in one sense independent of the physical part. Yet, in another way, it is very intimately connected. For example, you can plan precisely the way the shot should be made, and all of that thinking may be flawless. But the actual execution of the shot may fail completely because your physical ability to carry out the stroke has not measured up to your mental ability to conceive it.

The mental activity in golf involves mostly synthesis and control. Synthesis has to do with the planning of the swing. The control factor involves the emotional state of the mind. And, while it is true that there are certain fundamentals about the game that must be learned by every golfer, the understanding of these principles doesn't require any towering intellect. The big mental challenge in golf is thus in the area of *emotional control*. And it is here that many potentially great golfers have been destroyed—destroyed by their inability to handle their emotions.

Two emotions especially are difficult for the golfer to deal with. One is fear and the other is anger.

The fear is generally fear of inadequacy. The demands for precision in golf almost parallel those required in mathematics; these demands are so great that there is almost no margin for error. This kind of pressure is too great for most people, and they crumble under its unrelenting force. That's why it is so important for the golfer to understand as much as possible about *how* he must strike the ball. The more he understands each element of the physical action, the better he can implement the overall swing with absolute confidence, and thus the more easily he can overcome the fear of inadequacy.

It is the same stringent demand for precision that spawns the frustration leading to the anger so often displayed at every level of golf. I think golf causes more self-anger than any other sport, and in most instances this anger is simply the extreme form of a frustration that just can't be expressed in any other way.

Anger has driven people to some remarkable actions on the golf course. I had a professor of surgery in medical school who was said to have been one of the finest athletes in the country during his undergraduate days. One day he hit two successive balls into a water hazard on a short hole. Thereupon, he took his matched set of clubs and threw them one by one as far as he could out into the pond. He never played the game after that. This method of dealing with anger is hardly the most effective one, but it is a classic example of how the game can reduce a highly intelligent, well-controlled, and otherwise emotionally stable human being to a savage beast.

The problem here is the conflict created by two diametrically opposed concepts. You have on the one hand the mental formulation of the easiest way to move the golf ball from A to B, and on the other hand the extraordinary physical precision required to carry out that task. To reconcile the two requires simultaneously a great degree of confidence and an equal degree of humbleness—a mixture present in most of the greatest golfers of the past. Confidence comes from experience and a thorough knowledge of all aspects of the game. Humility also comes from experience, which teaches the golfer that he will always hit some bad shots; that 100 percent technical proficiency is impossible; that the game will win more often than he does.

THE AURA OF REVERENCE

THERE is implicit in the game of golf a deep sense of control that is difficult for many people to adopt or even accept. It is almost a religious quality, as though everyone involved in the game were participating in a sacred ritual. And the ritual *has* to be accepted, because people who depart from it are at first censored by the other participants and finally excommunicated.

Some of the high priests of golf do eventually, through the privileges that grow from success, acquire more liberty in this area than the general run of players. Lee Trevino, for example, clowns like a little boy who has brought his new toy to Sunday school. But how quickly he turns that clowning off when he addresses the ball.

Generally, this peculiar state of religiosity is always present, not only on occasions as celestial as the Masters Tournament, but in all "serious" golf—right on down to the $1 Nassau. The golfer who reacts against this aspect of the game eventually finds himself playing alone. Indeed, anyone who is not ready to play golf with this peculiar reverence is really not ready to play at all.

Even though this kind of statement infuriates the nongolfer, in that it smacks of fanaticism and elitism, there is a good sociological reason for it. In a modern technocratic society that takes away individual initiatives, this one activity stands firm like a rock, for everyone is equal on the golf course. There, the shipping clerk can for brief moments become superior to the chairman of the board. And if the spirit of the true golfer resides in the heart of the chairman of the board, he humbly bows to the man who may be considerably inferior to him in many other areas of life.

The "hooked" golfer can thus come to feel toward the game the same way that young lovers feel about each other. Golf invades every area of his life, gradually moving to the top of his hierarchy of values, offering an emotional experience that is almost spiritual in its quality. This experience can lock him to golf with an intensity that rarely exists in other games.

THE PHYSICAL CHALLENGE

FINALLY among golf's challenges there are the physical factors. Golf is certainly a very physical game, but it is physical in a very special way.

The golfer about to execute his shot is not unlike the diver who stands at the tip of the diving board contemplating the kind of maneuver he will execute. This maneuver is reviewed mentally with great care before execution. The mechanics and timing of all its aspects are fully understood. There is nothing spontaneous about the action itself. It is simply the end result of a final intellectual rehearsal.

But the golfer's experience is more complicated than that of the gymnast or diver. He not only has to perform precisely and with good timing a complex physical maneuver, but he has to perform it in such a way that the face of the club he holds in his hands contacts a very small ball within very fine limits at very high speed. The measure of excellence of the diver or the gymnast lies in the beauty and precision of his own physical maneuver. The excellence of the golfer's physical maneuver is judged by the fate of the ball itself, in that, no matter how beautifully the golfer swings, he has failed if the ball does not go to his intended target.

All of these factors make golf a very demanding game. And for this very different and difficult game, special mental as well as physical techniques are required. This book is about those mental techniques.

2

How Your Mind Works

THE golfer does not need a college course in the function and working of the mind in order to use it effectively. But he should understand some of the mind's fundamental operations, and certainly he should know how to apply that knowledge to his golf game.

The first problem most people face in understanding the mind is that they don't believe it is "real." Most people can believe only in things that have physical dimensions. You can't weigh a mind or stick it with a pin, and therefore, to many people, it cannot exist. They believe that the mind and the brain are synonymous, which is like saying that the electricity in a wire leading to a light bulb is the same as the light that shines from the bulb when the switch is thrown.

Light and electricity are different forms of energy. They are closely related in the situation just described, but each operates according to separate laws. The same is true of the mind and the brain. Since the mind is not "physical," it cannot be defined in terms of what it *is*, but rather in terms of what it *does*. But the golfer must recognize the mind as something that is as *real* and as *influential* in his game as his arms and legs.

The golfer should know that the mind does essentially two things: it thinks and it feels. Many educators like to compare the function of the mind to that of a computer. The analogy is applicable generally but weak in one particular area, because, although the computer thinks, and has a memory bank, and can solve problems by deductive logic, it cannot *feel*. If man's mind were simply a computer, there would be many more golfers breaking 80, but, interestingly enough, not 70. Later I'll tell you why this is so.

A major problem with the mind is that, although it can be programmed like a computer (i.e., think), its feelings can take over and totally destroy that logical programming (or thought) process. Many golfers have very clear-cut ideas about what they would like to do with the club and the ball, and very specific notions about how to carry it out. But if doubt or fear creeps into the system—in other words, the wrong sort of *feelings*—all their best-laid plans can be totally shattered.

BEING HONEST WITH YOURSELF

ON the whole, the golfer has much more trouble with the feeling function of the mind than with the thinking function. As we have stated, the intellectual problems in golf are not particularly great. But there is one such problem that all golfers have to face, and that is the assessment of their own capabilities in terms of their shot-making judgments.

Most golfers find it difficult to be truthful about themselves. People who play other games can generally own up to their ineptitude—they usually don't mind admitting they can't really play football, hockey, or basketball like a professional. But, for some strange reason, everybody *thinks* he should be able to play golf like Nicklaus.

On some snowy winter day, ask your bogeying friend what he shoots. If he has broken 90 twice in the past year, he'll tell you without batting an eye that he scores in the middle eighties. He knows that statement isn't true, but he thinks that by the time spring comes around he'll be shooting in the low eighties quite often, which means that his average score will by then be in the high eighties. In his own mind he's not really telling a lie; he's simply transposing the problem into the future. If you follow his progress closely, you may find that he actually doesn't break 100 until the middle of July. But, even at that point, he'll probably still think of himself as an eighties shooter. It is this subtle self-deception that prevents so many people from reaching an effective level of proficiency in golf.

A golfer should strive to be honest about his capabilities, no matter how humbling that experience may be. Because, without a firm footing of honesty, he will forever wallow in a quicksand of fantasy that must totally inhibit real and lasting improvement.

GOLF'S INTELLECTUAL PROBLEMS

ONCE he has learned to assess his capabilities honestly, the golfer is free to deal with the basic intellectual problem of how to play each hole in the least number of strokes. This would not be too difficult if he could count upon consistency with each club within a margin of, say, ten yards. But few golfers are that consistent.

The nonexpert golfer cannot hit the ball the same way every time. That's what he strives for, of course, but it simply doesn't happen, for two reasons: most golfers don't really understand the basic mechanics and dynamics of the golf swing, which means that their actions are not repetitive; and few golfers practice enough to ever achieve the physical precision and repeatability necessary for golfing excellence (understanding is not enough if you don't translate that understanding into actual performance).

A champion golfer once told me that only ten golfers in the world really know how to swing the golf club the right way. That's quite a statement, but the champion is quite a student of the game, and I'll respect anything that he tells me. Ignorance of the proper golf swing, then, is one of the major intellectual flaws of the average golfer.

The second purely intellectual problem of the inexpert golfer is his attitude toward success. He must use his mind to program his system for success with as much deliberation as he uses in placing his hands in a certain position on the club. Even when the percentage of success is slim, the golfer must still continue to intellectually program himself for it, even in the face of the most powerful emotional resistance.

Some people might feel that continuing to think success when you actually experience a high degree of failure is a form of self-destruction. The fact is that no golfer can ever achieve real success in the game unless he really believes in himself. Without such positive thinking, success will *never* follow.

One key to self-confidence is setting realistic targets —honestly analyzing your own capabilities and then believing in your ability to succeed at your own level. Even then, belief doesn't guarantee success, but without it, I repeat, success is impossible.

Belief in your ability to succeed at your level is thus the leading requirement in "the orchestra of the mind." Without this thought directing it, the orchestra deteriorates into discord, resulting in a game that is equally chaotic.

GOLF'S EMOTIONAL PROBLEMS

IF the golfer first can be honest about his capabilities, second can begin to understand and master the mechanics of the golf swing, and third can be positive in his approach to its execution, he is well on his way to success. Then it is not the intellectual factors that pose the challenge, but rather the problem of emotional control. The hard fact is that if the golfer can't control his emotions, golf is always going to cause him a lot of mental torture.

This is not to say that feelings themselves are undesirable. Without feelings man's experience would be extremely bland. Life would become a two-dimensional black and white movie. Feelings give life a richness and a depth that it could never have without them.

In actuality, because of the nature of the game, the golfer is generally more dependent upon his feelings than his intellect. For example, America's top golf teacher, Bob Toski, wrote a book called *The Touch System for Better Golf*, a system based upon feeling.

And most of the great golfers I know describe the golf swing as a feeling experience. If you ask them what they think about when they're swinging, the usual reply is "nothing much." They just "feel," and their execution of the golf swing is based upon that feeling.

Now, I recognize that this is an almost incomprehensible statement to a person who has never had the great golfer's feeling of the swing—it slams the door right in the face of the poor guy or girl who has never been there. But I hope to help solve this mystery during the course of this book by explaining *how* the great golfers feel what they do.

Intuition and feeling make man different from the computer. It is these special intuitive messages that are the key to the secret of our going beyond the mechanical capability of the computer. Golfers need intuition, along with intellect, to break 70. The totally intellectual golfer could never break 80. This doesn't mean that the golfer should not use his intellect, but in some ways the intellect isn't enough. It can be too metallic, too machine-like. Feeling and intuition are essential, *so long as they are used positively*.

Putting is an area where feelings play a really major role. All great putters have what is known as "touch." Putting ability is almost all intuitive. You could teach anybody with an I.Q. of 105 all the intellectual secrets of reading greens in eight hours or less, because these things are finite: the grain of the grass can influence the roll of the ball only in a certain number of ways; the contours of the green can have only certain specific effects upon the movement of the ball, etc. But the *knowledge* of these factors alone doesn't make a great putter. The key to his greatness lies in his magic "touch," which allows him to bring the putter blade through the ball in just the right way to implement what his intellect has told him about the speed and direction of the ball.

What is really in Nicklaus's mind when he crouches so long over a putt? You can be sure he's planned the shot long before he steps up to the ball, so he can't be thinking about the mechanics involved. What he's waiting for is that special feeling within himself that tells him he is ready to make the shot.

The right feelings, as well as the right intellectual approaches, are thus vital elements of the game.

If the right feelings can help to lift a golfer out of mediocrity, the wrong feelings can just as easily plunge him into, and keep him in, utter desolation. The most common feelings that do this are anger, fear, impatience, greed, and despair. These emotions can strike at any time, and the golfer must be able to anticipate, identify, and overcome them. He must recognize them as alien forces that, uncontrolled, can destroy his game in a flash.

FREUD IN GOLF

IN order to help the golfer better understand and handle these mysterious forces in his mind, it might be a good idea to consider briefly some of the fundamentals of dynamic mind functioning.

Sigmund Freud was the pioneer in this field. He recognized two spheres of mental activity, the conscious and the unconscious.

Everyone is aware of the activity of his conscious mind, the part that is directly in tune with reality as it unfolds moment by moment. This is the part of the mind that is connected to the senses, the things we smell, see, hear, taste, and touch. It arranges this information in a logical order that provides a meaning for each experience. It sees relationships between present and past events. Its ability to associate these experiences provides a depth of meaning that would not be possible without this function. Thus the conscious mind operates on the basis of logic. It is aware of certain underlying principles that influence physical life, such as gravity, time, and motion, and it respects these and operates within their limitations.

The conscious mind draws its conclusions from the obvious. For example, if a golfer is late for his match, his conscious mind might attribute this to the fact that, an hour before he was due to leave the office, he was suddenly swamped with work. His need to get that work done compelled him to be late. But the possibility also exists that some other factor is really what made him late. For example, it could be that one of the people in the foursome was somebody he did not much like, and being late was the only way he could register his objection. The point I am trying to make is that the conscious mind usually sees only what it wants to see and ignores what it doesn't want to see.

The other part of the mind, of whose activities we are not directly aware, is known in psychiatry as the unconscious mind. If the concept of mass could be applied to the mind, the unconscious mind would be much bigger than the conscious mind. Indeed, Freud likened the mind to an iceberg, in which the unconscious mind is that immense part of the iceberg lying below the water. The smaller part above the water, the tip of the iceberg, is the conscious mind.

Because we are not directly aware of the workings of the unconscious mind, they are more ominous than those of the conscious mind. The unconscious mind can infiltrate our conscious thinking and influence our behavior in ways that have nothing to do with our wills or intentions. Moreover, we have no real knowledge of the extensiveness of its action, in that its roots are deeply sunk in the most primitive instinctual experiences of our past development. Direct evidence of the unconscious mind is to be seen in such phenomena as dreams, slips of the tongue, and sudden strange, impulsive behavior that seems to have no basis in the person's environment at any given moment.

The golfer who *always* plays poorly on the first hole, or shanks on the same par-three hole every time, is under the influence of forces from his unconscious mind. He may try new grips, new methods, even new clubs, but all will be to no avail. In all such situations, the golfer's mistake arises as a result of his conscious mind being under the influence of his unconscious mind. And it was in his attempt to understand this kind of thing, and to put it into some kind of logical perspective, that Freud conceived of the anatomy of the mind.

GOLF AND THE ID

FREUD argued that the mind is composed of three repositories of mental activity, the Ego, the Superego, and the Id. Of these three, the Id is the basic mass of mind material out of which the other parts develop. The Id is therefore the most fundamental component of the mind and represents the raw material of the psyche.

We attribute to the Id's substance the activity of our instincts, those inner compulsive drives which are stimulated by certain environmental conditions. The most important instincts of the Id are the sexual and the aggressive, and a quick look at history will confirm the importance of these drives in man's experience.

The Id, then, as the center of instinctual behavior, is the powerhouse of the mind. It is capable of fantastic achievement, or of complete and utter destruction. In its raw, undiscriminating state, the Id obeys no laws and demands gratification as quickly as possible. It will not tolerate delay or modification but demands immediate straight-line fulfillment. It operates according to the "pleasure principle," all of its activity being directed toward giving the individual the greatest amount of instinctual gratification in the shortest amount of time. Id-oriented people are in bondage to a terrible tyrant. Indeed, when these impulses are not controlled, man becomes a slave to his instincts and eventually succumbs to them.

There is plenty of Id activity to be seen on the golf course. Let's just take one example. The chairman of the board of a bank, who has attained his respected position on the basis of keen intelligence, objectivity, and razor-sharp judgment, wraps his wedge around a tree trunk because he has shanked an easy pitch shot into a sand trap. If he'd given in to that kind of wildly impulsive behavior in his banking career, he'd still be sharpening pencils in the mail room, at best.

One way of handling the Id would be to completely stamp it out, but that would make the golfer a colorless machine. The golfer must therefore accept his Id as part of his mental make-up, while trying to understand it and to modify it to his needs through understanding. He must never forget that the Id will always be there. But he must at the same time be willing to take precautions and make provisions for this unpredictable part of his personality—remembering that, once his Id is in the saddle, he is in for a very rough ride indeed on the golf course.

Two other parts of the mind function as modifying influences on the undisciplined energy sources of the Id. One of these is called the Ego and the other the Superego.

GOLF AND THE EGO

THE Ego is not to be confused with the meaning of the word "ego" in popular usage, indicating a person's exalted opinion of himself. This definition is a far cry from the meaning of the word as it is used in psychiatry, where the Ego is understood to be the part of the mind that organizes a person's psyche into a specific shape. And it is not only an organizer, but also a mediator. The word "ego" will be used both ways in this book. Freud's Ego will be capitalized.

We saw the Id as a shapeless, disorganized mass of psychic energy that explodes in unpredictable ways. The function of the Ego is to take that raw material and to mold it into a highly adaptable personality, capable not only of meeting the demands and exigencies of life, but of fulfilling its own creative capabilities.

The specific functions of the Ego are perception, association, abstraction, analysis, synthesis, and memory. The Ego is an activist. It provides controls so that a person can condition himself to meet any task. The Ego does this through the acquisition of understanding, the gaining of wisdom, and the communication of knowledge.

A healthy Ego makes a golfer use a 5 iron on a hole where his companions may be using 7 or 8 irons, because he knows from his own experience and capabilities that for him the 5 iron is the best club for the job. The Id, of course, would have him hit a wedge when everyone else was using a 2 iron, to show how strong and powerful he really is.

The Ego disciplines itself not because of the imposition of external authority, but because of internal controls. A golfer with a healthy Ego is ready to meet any task that might confront him. If, for example, he finds a ball in a difficult lie, he doesn't automatically try to improve the lie with his foot (Id activity), but accepts the challenge of the situation, and reaches into his creative potential to find a solution. The person with a healthy Ego doesn't consciously distort the truth, because what he actually wants is to *know* the truth so that he can base his actions upon facts and his own capabilities.

The Ego, however, like any other living entity, can be affected by alien forces. Its greatest enemy is fear, and it is out of fear that the Ego unconsciously develops defense mechanisms. These mechanisms are developed in order to protect the individual from certain aspects of reality that he considers to be destructive. They are his primitive way of checkmating fear. At worst they are forms of self-deception. At best they provide attitudes that encourage him to venture into areas of experience that he may basically fear.

One of the principal Ego defense mechanisms is "repression"—the mental mechanism that enables the mind to eliminate an intolerable episode from the consciousness by plunging the experience so deeply into the unconscious that the person is not aware of it and therefore not afraid of it. "Out of sight, out of mind" is a principle that mankind has been practicing for a long time!

It takes energy to repress material into the unconscious, and that energy-laden material has a way of erupting into the conscious mind at inappropriate times. A golfer may feel a great hostility toward, and contempt for, putting, but experience forces him to recognize the importance of this aspect of the game. He knows he will never be an accomplished golfer until he has mastered it. He therefore represses his hostility and gives lip service to the importance of the putting part of the game.

However, if you happen to observe such a person closely, you will find that he *never* practices on the putting green. Instead, he's always to be found on the driving range, looking for extra yardage with his woods or greater accuracy with his irons. On the course, he's long with the woods, keen with the irons, but he uses his putter with all the delicacy of a bull in a china shop, his hostility erupting in the form of atrocious putts that immediately cancel any advantage that he may have gained from his expert shots to the green.

Another common defense mechanism used by everyone, and often seen on the golf course, is that of "projection." We project to other people the weaknesses, defects, and personality failings that we don't want to accept within ourselves.

For example, most golfers have problems at some time or other with the "killer instinct," an uncontrol-

that moment, it is obvious that the golfer
driver in some way had something to do wi
shot. In the act of slamming it down,
reverts to the type of behavior that
childhood. The golfer doesn't often
a frustrating occurrence on th
does slam his club down hard
ground, or in fantasy fling
in all these instances h
misdeed.

This brings to
known as "ratio
guage, "makin
golf course
body or
he sh
iron

call "regression." Very often regression goes all the way back to childhood, as we revert to behavior that may have been appropriate at moments of stress in our development. In infancy and childhood, frustrating circumstances are usually met with anger, the child not having matured enough to control his emotions. Anger demands destruction, so the frustrated child will throw his bowl of food onto the floor and break the dish. That act of destruction releases the emotional tension within the child: he claps his hands with joy. Needless to say, it does something else to the mother, but that's another story!

It's common on the golf course to see a person slam his club to the ground after he's made a bad shot. At

eels his
th the poor
e temporarily
prevailed in his
throw dishes after
golf course, but he
nto the bag, or kick the
his club over a tree. And
is blaming the club for the

ind another defense mechanism
alization," or, in nontechnical lan-
excuses." This is very common on the
We all know the golfer who blames every-
everything but himself for his missed shots:
nked the 4 iron into the water because "the 4
is a lousy club, I should have used the 5 wood,"
nd so on. Actually, there was almost certainly nothing
wrong with the 4 iron, but there was a great deal wrong
with the way the golfer used it.

The rationalizer blames his misjudged putt on the
fact that the grass on the green was cut too short or
too long. He always sees himself as the victim of inexorable forces beyond his control; he can never recognize himself as being at fault. His whole life is spent
in passing the buck.

Then there is "transference," an unconscious process
whereby the golfer transfers to people in his present
environment emotional responses that pertain to certain specific people he has encountered in the past.

For example, the golfer may be overawed by an aggressive opponent who reminds him of a bully who
frightened him as a child. His mind can then become
so full of destructive fantasies about the opponent

that it destroys his own game. The golfer is not consciously aware of this transference or association: he is only aware of a gnawing sense of uneasiness and of the disturbing fact that, for some unknown reason, his game is deteriorating rapidly.

The golfer may unconsciously transfer to his teaching professional the demanding or unsympathetic attitude of a father, and his resulting fear and hostility may then eliminate any chance for him to benefit from the learning experience. Or he may find himself trying so hard to please the professional, in order to gain some form of approval, that any objective attempt to learn something about the game for his own gratification goes by the board.

The last defense mechanism that should be discussed is "identification." This is a mechanism whereby we imitate in our behavior the behavior of somebody else.

The learning golfer watches his professional coach swing the club, then tries to imitate him. That is positive identification—it's almost as if he were allowing the pro to swing for him until he has developed his own style. This type of identification plays an important role in any learning process.

Positive identification is often difficult for older golfers, but the fertile imagination of most youngsters allows them easily to become Johnny Millers or Tom Watsons in their own minds. That's why young people learn the game so much faster and generally more effectively than older people: their meager life experience doesn't allow them to become involved in negative identification.

Older people are natural candidates for negative identification. For example, the man who played a lot of baseball as a kid can't help but identify the golf swing with the swing of a baseball bat, especially if he was a good hitter. In learning golf, he wants to use his wrists and hands as he did when swinging the bat. It's frustrating for him when he doesn't get the same kind of results, and very difficult for him to accept and learn how different the golf swing is from any other swing he has used effectively in the past. If he can't break away from the earlier identification, his golf swing will simply be a modified baseball swing, and he will never know the special experience of the true golf swing.

GOLF AND THE SUPEREGO

THIS brings us to the third component of the mind as conceived by Freud—the Superego.

The Superego comes into being by the process of incorporation, in that it results from the absorption of the moral codes and prejudices of authority by which mankind abides. This absorption takes place for many reasons.

First, principles of behavior are forced upon a child directly by the parents and by others in authority over him. The child knows that obeying these dicta is one way to obtain love from his parents; rebelling against them causes anger and rejection, which the developing infant shies away from. However, if a child gets caught in a rejection pattern, he may assume rejection as a life style. The person who is a continual loser develops from this kind of experience. He's the person who always comes in second, not because he lacks the ability to win, but because he seems to court disaster and defeat. We'll go into this in more detail later on.

The Superego is an open enemy of the Id, in that it is unrelenting in its adherence to its principles. If our Superegos were to reign unchecked, we would be totally inhibited human automatons. The Superego is thus a good adjunct to help the Ego control certain aspects of Id behavior, which it would be unable to do without this kind of reinforcement.

THE MIND IS "REAL"

WE are, of course, barely scratching the surface in this limited description of the function of the mind and its anatomy. The aim here is merely to give the golfer enough knowledge to recognize that, when we talk about a mind, we are talking about something very *real*. We are, indeed, talking about a mechanism that can make or break our golf games. The mind is *not* simply the figment of the "shrink's" imagination.

Golfers who understand their minds, and who use them in the right way, are the golfers who play to the best of their ability. Indeed, this is true of all sport. It is tragic to see—as one so often does—a finely endowed athlete with an encyclopedic knowledge of the mechanics of a game destroy his chances of success because of his total ignorance of the operation of his mind. You can see this happening repeatedly in pro golf tournaments when players make bad shots, then review the picture of the shots in their minds and play them over with practice swings, obviously believing that the error was due to some improper physical action. It rarely occurs to such players that, during the swing, something might have happened in their *minds* to cause a sudden reflex contraction in some part of the body such as the hands, hips, or legs. Often this is exactly what did happen.

I hope this book will offer golfers another dimension to consider in trying to solve their playing problems. If the mind is, indeed, 90 percent of the game, as so many great golfers seem to think, then the average golfer should certainly find out all he can about its function and see how he can use that knowledge in the development and improvement of his game.

3

How Your Mind Makes You
the Kind of Golfer You Are

ALISTAIR COOKE once wrote an amusing article
about golf in the *New York Times*, entitled "Self-
torture Disguised as a Game." In it he makes this remarkable statement: "For of all forms of· exercise
theoretically designed for recreation and relaxation,
none can be so unerringly guaranteed to produce
nervous exhaustion and despair leading to severe
mental illness· and in some cases petulance."

There is no doubt that golf, with all its potential for
psychic torture, can distort the mind into many unsightly forms. The primary reason is that, on the
course itself, the mind can find no way to cover up the
inherent flaws in human nature. Therefore, instead of
freeing a man from the demons that drive him in other
areas of life, golf all too often opens the floodgates even
wider by compelling him to act out in public many of
the fears he so skillfully covers up elsewhere.

It is almost impossible to conceal your secret self on
a golf course. There are simply no psychological hiding

places—no way of concealing your lack of skill. A man who is nice to his work companions can become a dragon on the links as he runs headlong into his own ineptitudes. A man may be an all-American halfback in football, but that means nothing on a golf course. There, you either know how to play golf or you don't—and, either way, it will show.

Implicit in the game, therefore, is a kind of human vulnerability, since a player is forced to be honest with himself and to show himself honestly to others—even though he may hate to do so. That's why the game is so correctly known as a "test of character"; why people so rightly say that you can get to know more about a man during a round of golf than you can in a lifetime of seeing him in other circumstances.

Now, it is in man's nature to struggle against this harsh confrontation with himself, and from this struggle come the personality types that sometimes make the golf course look like a museum of psychopathology.

THE ANXIOUS GOLFER

EVERY golfer must deal with anxiety, but some people are so totally consumed by it that, on the course, their personalities are distorted into a specific form that we might call the "anxious type."

The anxious golfer always seems to be in a constant state of motion. He is endlessly active in greater or lesser ways. As he awaits his turn on the tee, he's hitching up his pants, retying his shoes, adjusting his belt. He's always wondering if his ball is quite clean enough. He's forever gripping his club, looking hard at the placement of his hands as though he'd never seen them in just that position before. He seems to be caught up by an endless stream of internal energy that demands immediate dissipation. He acts like a cornered animal not quite sure where to move next.

Finally, when his turn eventually comes, the anxious golfer hurries onto the tee as though pursued by demons, giving the impression that he simply cannot wait a second longer to hit his drive. He digs the tee viciously into the ground, glances quickly up the fairway, then just as quickly glances down at the ball, as though it were his nemesis rather than his ally. His companions watch with bated breath, because he seems almost at the point of explosion. He assumes his stance quickly and then even more quickly strikes the ball—in fact so quickly that, if you don't watch carefully, you may miss the action altogether. Then, as quickly as he ascended the tee, he rushes from it. He has his tee in his pocket and is stepping into the golf car before his ball comes to rest. You get the feeling he never saw where the ball went, but you can be very sure he did. If you play with him often enough, you may begin to understand that he doesn't need to follow his ball in flight because he repeats the same disaster shots over and over again. He knows exactly where the ball is going, even though it's never where he'd intended it should go.

The most puzzling thing about the anxious golfer is that he seems entirely unaware of his own agitation. You would think that when something is so patently obvious to others, it would be painfully obvious to the victim. Such, however, is not the case. Anxious golfers are almost totally under the influence of their anxiety —completely helpless in its grasp.

If you follow the anxious golfer down the fairway,

you will perceive that he moves at the same driven pace that characterizes his behavior on the tee. He carries a club with him because he likes the feel of its whip-like presence in his hand. He swings it occasionally at the top of the short-clipped grass, deriving from this ritual some outlet for the relentless fire within him.

He quickly chooses a club for the shot at hand, but just as quickly he changes his mind, sometimes making three or four choices before he settles on the right one. This indecision is not due to any difficulty in judging distance, but rather is caused by fear of his inability to execute the shot. To the anxious type all hazards are fraught with danger. Sand traps turn his muscles to jelly. Water hazards paralyze every nerve in his body. He attempts to bypass both with wild detours, sacrificing one shot, even two, to avoid any confrontation with these monsters dreamed up by some golfing Franken-stein.

His antics on the green parallel his behavior on the tee. He fidgets over the ball, his mind seemingly blind to all but one thought—to hit the ball as quickly as possible. Attaining his putting stance is agonizing, as if he is punishing himself for the sin of stupidity he is shortly to commit. The putter seems so charged with electricity that you feel it's going to leap out of his hands if he doesn't hold it in a vise-like grip. When he finally drops the ball into the hole, he quickly retrieves it and steals off the green to resume his unbridled "fidgetry" on the next tee.

If you were to follow such a golfer into other areas of his life, you would see the same anxiety that drives him on the golf course still relentlessly pursuing him. His pace at the office is frenetic, showing the same lack of awareness of his hyperactivity. His subordinates flinch before his relentless, undisciplined energy, and his superiors worry about him. He makes the latter nervous too, even though they know that any job they give him to do will be done well.

There is something almost indecent about this amount of nervousness, for it is unappealing to witness human emotional flaws hanging out with such complete abandon. And the really sad thing is that golf, of all pastimes, could bring great relief to this tortured soul, if only he could deal with its challenges in the right way; in a way that we'll talk about later on.

THE ANGRY GOLFER

AND then there's the angry type. . . .

The angry golfer may start out in a perfectly equable mood. If all goes well for the first three or four holes, you may think that he's one of the nicest, most stable persons you've ever played with. But, as the game progresses, and if you are perceptive, you will begin to notice a gradual mounting of tension. It never reaches the shanking palsy symptoms of the anxious type—it might never reveal itself in more than a change in the timbre of his voice or the pace of his walk—but the mounting tension is there and recognizable in the "vibes" the golfer gives off.

Here is a golfer who is waiting. He's waiting for that fatal error he *knows* must sooner or later strike him cruelly and quickly. The blow can come at any time and in any way. Let's say it occurs in the form of a muffed pitch from a perfect lie. Instead of landing a few feet from the cup in birdie territory, the ball buries in

a bunker. Immediately before your eyes Dr. Jekyll will
turn into Mr. Hyde. The first thing you will notice is an
expression of rage transforming his face.

It goes without saying that there is no way to console such a golfer at this point. For one thing, he
couldn't hear you. His internal rage is so consuming
that it deafens his ear to any sound from without. It's
almost as if suddenly all living things were alien to his
tortured mind. People become inanimate objects. His
one compelling desire is to destroy something.

This is a form of unbridled animal aggression. The
Id is running wild. The golfer has become an enraged
child who has lost his object of love. His only con-
solation is to destroy. In this instance, the target of this
destructive force is the ball that has found its way into
the treacherous sand. The player jerks his sand-wedge
violently from the bag, like a sword from a tight
sheath. He wrestles his feet viciously deep into the
sand. Gone from his mind are all niceties of technique.
His Superego has withered to the size of a mustard
seed. His mind is interested in one thing and one thing
only: annihilating the ball that his rapidly regressing
mind has cast as the villain of the piece.

He swings hard and fast. The only golf-related
thought in his head is the word "blast." So blast he
does—and how! Sand volcanically erupts toward the
green, but the ball catches the lip of the hazard and
resolutely trickles right back into the pit.

Now, tormented almost beyond bearing, all the
golfer wants to do is leap at the ball and beat it into a
thousand pieces. But suddenly he senses that several
silent pairs of eyes are carefully—perhaps critically—
watching his every move. So he strikes again, but this
time a bit more carefully. His awareness of that silent

audience has helped him to contain some of the explosiveness of his rage, and the resulting semicontrolled shot drops the ball somewhere on the green. Still, the roots of destruction have dug too deeply into the earth of his mind for him to continue to play golf with any logic. From then until the end of the round, his challenge will no longer be golf, but self-containment—the Ego and Superego fighting for their lives against the Id.

The angry golfer's game is now characterized by the spirit of defeatism. The other members of the group know that they are playing with a lost soul. The spirit of defeat prevails, hanging like a dark cloud over their companion and often permeating the attitude, and therefore the play, of the entire group. Only the end of the game brings relief to this symphony of rage. The possessed one heads quickly for the bar and there tries to drown as quickly as possible the smoldering coals of his deadly anger.

THE JOKER

THEN we have the joker, the guy who wants to make light of everything.

To some people, an externally light-hearted demeanor is a great defense against anxiety. Lee Trevino is the greatest living example of this type of golfer, but Trevino makes this trait work *for*, rather than *against*, him. He's funny all the time except when he stands over the ball. At that point he becomes very serious, very intense, and this intensity and concentration continue until he is finished with his commitment to the ball. Without the mental flexibility that lets him become serious over the ball, Trevino couldn't break 80.

The *true* joker tries to be funny *all* the time on the course, but *especially* when he is over the ball. He has to make the game a comedy. He's more comfortable with laughter than tears. But beneath the clown's mask is the tragic countenance of a man who is not being honest with himself.

The joker is a pathetic figure because he is unaware of his own deceitfulness. He operates on the principle that if you can laugh at something then you no longer need to fear it. But his laughter prevents him, in many instances, from even beginning to play the game competently. And no serious golfer who knows him wants to play with him. His defenses are too pathetically transparent, and most people wince when they get him for a partner.

To describe him at his worst, the true joker is a coward because he is afraid to put himself on the line. His rationalization goes something like this: "If I half try and miss then I still know that, if I *really* tried, I could do it."

Playing with a joker seems fun at first, because it takes some of the tension out of the game. But there comes a time when you wish the levity would cease, because eventually the concentration and commitment of all the other players in the group will be affected. At that point, what has begun as good-natured tolerance of the joker ends in diminished respect for him.

Frequently, the joker's comedy is an emotional manifestation of his inner lack of respect for himself. He knows he's a coward, but naturally he doesn't want to face that fact. He laughs at the slice that careens off into the woods, which is at first a refreshing change from the charged atmosphere created by the angry golfer. But when the triviality is repeated again and again, it becomes embarrassing.

The angry type is at least a lot more honest with himself than the joker, and to that degree you can respect him. But the true golfer despises the joker and avoids him, even if he's basically a nice guy, because his lack of respect for the game is contagious. It breeds carelessness and lack of concentration, which the serious golfer wants to avoid. He cannot afford these human frailties.

Ultimately this feeling of aversion seeps through the joker's elephant-thick skin. He is seen less and less around the club. Eventually you hear that he's taken up tennis, and, if you wonder about him at all, you wonder how many laughs he's getting on the courts.

THE BIG HITTER

AND then we have the big hitter.

Here's the guy who plays golf only to outdrive everybody else by seventy-five yards, the fellow who loves to use an 8 iron when everybody else is using a 4. Actually, he's not really a golfer but a human cannon: a projector of missiles over long distances. He doesn't care all that much about scoring well. He just wants it to be known that he can outhit everyone else on the course.

There is often an electrifying flamboyance about this golfer, but also a pathos that escapes most people. He's like a fish out of water. His natural habitat is the driving range, where less stringent demands are made upon precision. Everyone is impressed by his Goliath-like strength, finding it incredible that any man should be using a pitching wedge for his second shot on, say, a 440-yard hole. A wedge is designed to lift and place, not to smash. But the big hitter swings his wedge with the same abandon as he does his driver. You can almost feel the earth shudder when he lashes through the turf. A huge divot ascends into the sky like a cloud. The ball flies so high that you think it might breed icicles.

The big hitter loves to backspin these shots viciously, the amount of spin again being a measure of his Herculean strength. He is unconcerned that the spin backs the ball six feet shorter of the hole. His pleasure lies almost entirely in displaying his great strength.

Where the pathos really shows through is when the big hitter gets to the green. He detests everything about that closely clipped carpet of grass. The delicate touch it calls for revolts him. The putter, that puny little stick possessing no inherent power, disgusts him. He lines up his putt very quickly and hits it with a speed that tells you he wants to get this nonsense over, so he can move on to the tee again, where men are men. As he snatches his ball from the hole and races off the green in disgust, you can almost read everybody's mind: "If this guy could only putt he'd be a scratch player." But somehow you know it isn't going to be, and you almost feel sorry for him, because it seems such a waste of talent. You know that if *you* could hit the ball fifty yards farther you'd be shooting in the seventies, but you know that this fellow is never going to get the message. He gets his kicks another way.

Until the process of aging catches him, the big hitter will usually always be the big hitter. I've never looked into the fate of big hitters when they get old, but I suspect that they never really change, even when arthritic degeneration won't let them take the club

back any farther than Doug Sanders punching a
wedge.

THE LEGAL TYPE

PLAYING with the legal type can be one of the
most exasperating experiences in golf. He may not be
skillful in terms of shot making, but when it comes to
the rules he's your all-time expert.

The legal type is usually the first of the group to
arrive at the first tee, but instead of going through a
ritual of warm-up exercises like most golfers do, he
carefully studies all the written material on the scorecard, even though he must have read it at least a
hundred times before. He's keenly aware of the handicap holes, and you can be sure he knows where he'll be
giving or getting shots from you, and everyone else
in the club. He knows the exact stroke penalties for
water hazards and out of bounds. He can quote you
local rules word for word. Above all, he loves to keep
score.

Another interesting thing about this type of golfer is
that he knows exactly what every player in the group
makes on every hole. If you're not sure whether you're
shooting your fourth or fifth shot, ask the legalist—*he*
will know. Other golfers are often a little timid about
telling him their scores at the end of each hole, because
they are never quite sure they will coincide with the
calculations of this mobile computer.

When there is a disagreement, the legalist registers
the discrepancy in one of two ways. Either he is openly
adamant—the kind that could send an impoverished

widow to the poorhouse without a quiver of compassion
—in which case he'll tell you frankly that he's got you
down for six even though you've told him five. Or he
becomes quietly severe and suspicious-looking, never
quite expressing his disbelief in words, but rather
through a slightly raised brow or a quick pursing of the
mouth. Such expressions, as they are intended to, strike
deep into the soul of the accused. The full moral weight
of the situation descends on his shoulders. He begins to
wonder if he did not, indeed, forget a stroke, or even
whether he was, in fact, deliberately trying to cheat.

Such experiences can throw a golfer's whole game
out of whack. You are expected to keep your own scores
honestly, and if there is any doubt about your ability to
do so, inevitably you are under suspicion for the rest of
the round—and perhaps forever. Stating your score
at the finish of each hole thus becomes a tense moment,
and, given the chance, you will avoid the legal type as
a future golfing companion.

THE ILLEGAL TYPE

BECAUSE golf's idealistic honor system is sometimes too demanding for the human psyche, we occasionally run across the type of golfer that can be
designated "illegal." The illegal golfer is rarely evil: it's
just that the game puts too much strain on his mind—
a mind already too aware of its own frailties. The illegal
golfer is simply a moral weakling.

This type of golfer rarely loses a ball, though he
frequently knocks them into the woods. He very often

finds his ball in a place quite remote from the likely area ascertained by others. Invariably its lie will be good.

Whereas the legal type has an almost encyclopedic knowledge of the actual Rules of Golf, the illegal type has a tendency to make his own rules as he goes along. He never reads the printed material on the back of the scorecard. He assumes that local rules offering relief are in effect even when they are not. He plays "winter rules" all year round. He never gives himself more than *one* stroke penalty, no matter what the situation. He feels that having to drop another ball is sufficient penalty in itself—why gild the lily?

This philosophy has a certain simplistic appeal that cannot be denied, but it is always a source of intense irritation to other members of the foursome who pride themselves on their honesty and who respect the game as it is, not as they might like it to be.

The remarkable thing about these illegal golfers is that they really don't believe they are doing anything wrong. To them, all is fair in love, war, and golf. If in the course of a game they have knocked five strokes off their average score, they feel no compunction about taking money from their losing opponents. They forget their infractions as quickly and as easily as they make them.

This type of golfer may be scrupulously honest in other areas of his life, but there is something about the intense moral stress of golf that withers his ethical timbers. An honest, upright, law-abiding citizen off the course can become a devious, underhanded embezzler once he steps on the first tee. And, most peculiar of all, he never seems to understand that the person he is cheating most is himself.

THE EXHIBITIONIST

THE exhibitionist is a type very common to golf. His clothing is generally brilliant, with the colors often mixed in a manner that dazzles the eye. He swaggers like a peacock out for a stroll in the afternoon sun. He's intensely aware of his every move. He obviously enjoys the impression he makes.

In a way these jaunty peacocks are a harmless and refreshing addition to the color and appeal of the game. They relieve its underlying grimness; dating back to its Gaelic origins and still reflected in the somber dress of most golfers in Scotland, where grays, browns, and blacks still predominate, and where applause for even the greatest shots at British Opens is still restrained and circumspect.

Today, there is a general trend toward brighter colors, but the exhibitionist goes beyond this, not only in his apparel but in the way he plays the game. The exhibitionist has a strong sense of the dramatic. He loves nothing better than to stand center stage on the tee, performing within the full brilliance of the spotlight. Nothing is dearer to his heart than the "oohs" and "aahs" of the audience. And for this reason, you can always bet he's going for the long ball.

The exhibitionist never takes the easy way home. If there's a short cut over the trees, that's the way he will go. Unfortunately, his skill does not always match his grandiosity, and therefore he often finds himself in deep trouble. But even this does not quench his ebullience, for he loves the dramatic potential of situations that would strike terror into the heart of most golfers.

There's something immensely attractive about any

human activity that courts disaster, as witnessed by the massive interest in, and following of, people like Evel Knievel. Sensing this, the exhibitionist will always take the suicide route; the safe way is fundamentally repugnant to his nature. The possibility of dropping a couple of extra strokes doesn't bother him in the least, when weighed against the possibility of the applause and approbation that he craves.

Even the putting green, that ultimate leveler of all beings, does not quell this man's indomitable spirit. He "goes" for every putt. He will not dampen his dramatic flair with the word "lag." Whether the putt is six feet or sixty, he always tries to hole it. His motto is "never up, never in." And he is always up, but seldom in.

THE HUSTLER

HUSTLING exists in every area of human activity, but there may be more out-and-out hustlers in golf than in any other sport.

It is never very difficult to spot the true hustler, because there's absolutely nothing he won't bet on. It would be sacrilegious for him to play a game of golf without some real money hanging in the balance.

The hustler is usually a pretty good golfer, because he plays a lot and he plays for keeps. He is, however, rarely a real student of the game. He seldom practices but simply plays enough—and under enough self-imposed pressure—to maintain his form. His chief thrill on the links, as in most other areas of life, lies in turning a quick buck.

While rarely a real student of the game itself, the

hustler is a connoisseur of the other types that play it.
He can spot a phony in half a second and likes nothing
better than to get a "pigeon" to play two or three strokes
below his handicap. Any hesitancy shown by a prospect
in stating his handicap is a green light to the hustler.
He loves statements like: "Well, I usually play between
12 and 15." You can be sure that the fluctuator will be
playing to a 12 or less—and feeling good about it.

The hustler, however, is totally aware of his own
capabilities, and nothing can make him deviate from
his own handicap. Thus he is generally extremely honest about himself. He knows his limitations and is
quick to admit them. His modesty is something over-
whelming. He will play with as high a handicap as you
are willing to give him.

The hustler does not have the true golfer's deep
commitment to the game—that enslavement to golf
that can seep into every aspect of many people's lives
until the game becomes their number one priority. Such
obsession never taints the mind of the hustler. His
greatest thrill lies not in hitting a ball 250 yards
straight as an arrow—he can't apply any monetary
value to that experience—but in what his good shots
will win for him.

THE LOSER

"ALL the world loves a winner." But what about
the poor loser?

What the world feels for losers is basically contempt.
Yet, they abound on any course. They are recognizable
by a penchant for losing that transcends their natural
abilities. Some of the finest natural golfers I know

are losers. It would seem there's something about success that threatens them. They derive a definite comfort from finishing second, if not last.

The loser can look like a champion for twelve holes. Then something always happens to his game. His swing still looks the same, but for some mysterious reason his shots begin to stray off target. Once this process begins, it gathers momentum like a snowball rolling down a hillside. One almost gets the feeling that the fellow's deliberately not trying. But why would a person put himself into this humiliating position? Does anyone *really* want to be despised? What is so terrible about being a winner?

The truth is that the world may love winners, but their lives—as the top tournament pros know—are not all roses and honey. They are king of the castle now, but everyone is pounding at the castle gate. When you're a loser, nobody wants your place. When you're a winner, everybody does. Winners know their glory will generally be short-lived—they have to *keep on* winning to stay on top. Winners are lonely.

The tragedy of the loser is that often he has the equipment to become a winner, but, because of some psychological flaw, he cannot (or will not) allow that potential to materialize. Often the problem is too subjective an involvement with the game—a feeling that one's worth as a human being will be measured in terms of success at a game, and a revulsion against this criticism of worth. Such a person wants to be accepted for what he *is*, not for what he can *do*. Therefore he won't let himself win, because if he wins, he will be accepted as a human being on that basis. If a loser could develop an objectivity independent of his ego needs, he wouldn't be a loser any more. However, the transition rarely takes place, so deep-seated is the infantile need for recognition beyond that derived from achievement.

As the loser becomes more skillful at golf, he often becomes equally skillful in his ability to lose. It's comparatively easy to lose if you are an unskilled player, but it takes a unique kind of skill to lose if you're actually a good player. The loser has the innate capacity to do just that. His greatest pleasure comes from seeing how close he can get to the winners' circle without entering its deadly circumference.

These are just a few of the types to be seen on the golf course, where the psychological soil is so rich that it can generate any kind of behavior. But, in general terms, there is no doubt that most people perform as golfers according to their basic personalities. They display on the links in an overt form the same personality traits that they are able to hide in less vulnerable human experiences.

However, no golfer need be a slave to himself. Whatever his basic personality may be, if he understands it he can make it work for, rather than against, him on the golf course, and anywhere else. Indeed, this adjustment can be the richest part of the whole golf experience, in that people who come to grips with their personality flaws through golf can gain momentum that will help them to better handle those same problems in other aspects of their lives.

In this perspective golf is truly a microcosm of life, and from it the aware golfer can derive much more than a low handicap. Unfortunately, such is the potential of this game to totally saturate the human mind that for many golfers life is a microcosm of golf.

4

Golf's Major Mental Challenges

T HE great golfer is psychologically flexible. He owes much of his success to his ability to treat each situation on the golf course—good, bad, or average— with the same degree of concentration and respect. Unfortunately, few golfers have or seek to acquire this talent, and its lack is a major cause of their ineffectiveness.

A case in point is the golfer who can drive the ball great distances but has less interest in, or respect for, iron shots, and who may feel utter contempt for chipping or putting, or both. To such a man the great pleasure of golf lies in hitting the ball twenty-five yards farther than anybody else. But the truth is that he is not really playing *golf* at all—he's playing long-driving to satisfy his aggressive impulses. Often, such a person doesn't even begin to understand the full scope of golf. He would probably have a lot more fun if he simply stayed on the driving range. Yet, if this individual could learn to treat all the elements of golf with the kind of respect he shows for driving, he would have an excellent chance of becoming a good player, because—as his long drives prove—he definitely has the physical skills demanded by golf.

To another kind of person, the short game is the all-important facet of golf. Such golfers usually have the opportunity to become good scorers, but they could become even better if they did not neglect the long game. Frequently, there seems to be something fatalistic in their attitudes toward the power aspects of the game. They are so overawed by the myth of the big hitter that they are afraid to achieve their own distance potential. They play stuffily and overcautiously as a result.

The good golfer seeks the optimum return for his efforts in *every* situation. He respects all facets of the game equally. He accepts the uniqueness of each situation he faces on the course and is ready to meet each specific challenge on its merits, by calling on all his physical and mental powers.

The permutations obviously are endless, but there are basic situations in golf that represent common psychological challenges and that produce many conflicts. Let us examine some of these in the hope that, by clearly identifying them, we can better recognize and deal with them.

THE DRIVE

TO some extent the golfer is always on stage, but on the tee he is under the full force of the spotlight.

Standing on the tee is, indeed, not unlike being on a real stage—a very frightening experience for most people. The tee is elevated, and the audience stands around, their silence confirming their fixed attention upon every move of the performer. The ball is teed to his choice, and on level ground, making it relatively easy to hit—and thereby giving the golfer even less excuse for failure. In short, all the forces that produce stage fright are there. At such a moment everyone wants to excel, but, with the spotlight upon him, the golfer knows that there is no way he can conceal any mistakes he might make.

In this situation many golfers feel such an intense awareness of their weaknesses that they totally over-look their strengths. And, overriding everything, is the terror of appearing a fool. In combination, these two emotions open the floodgates for all kinds of negative ideas and actions. Feelings of awkwardness and in-competence move in, and, as the tension mounts, cerebral functioning becomes increasingly blunted. Eventually the mind regresses to the primitive stage where all responses are directed toward the immediate removal of pain and discomfort: the agony becomes so intense that the need for relief is immediate. All that matters then is to swing the club as quickly as possible to escape the cruel limelight.

We've all seen, and maybe experienced, this hu-miliating situation and watched helplessly as the ball trickles off the front of the tee or flies way off line into some dreadful grave. The golfer then retreats from center stage feeling a mixture of both anger and despair.

An even greater psychic pitfall of the drive lies not so much in the golfer being stage-center, but in the frailty of human nature as it confronts the *power myth*.

As the golfer stands in the middle of that grassy stage, looking over the beautiful landscape before him, he may become filled with a strange sense of power and omnipotence. The design of the course stimulates this feeling of grandiosity. The endless perspective of the landscape invites him into an infinite world, transcending the world of reality. These unconscious feelings infiltrate the golfer's system. The propulsive muscles are stimulated and stand alert, ready to enter the fray. The driver becomes a reenactment of the ritual of Superman. The impending demonstration of power draws admiration from the silent audience, who, once it is unleashed, will add with their flattering remarks verbal frosting to a cake already sweet. To the infinity that lies before him, the golfer now wishes to add the transcendence of the ball.

This, of course, is a drift away from reality, and in the game of golf any deviation from reality is dangerous. But the power myth is so dominant that it can override any other cerebral function.

Some golfers never overcome their susceptibility to the power myth. It dominates their activity in every situation on the golf course, even when they are playing comparatively short shots where delicacy is the main requirement. These are the golfers who *always* take a 7 iron where they really need a 5 iron, and who *always* hit everything flat out.

All golfers must be aware of this susceptibility, for only by being aware of it and its devastating effects can they do anything about controlling it.

Control lies in overcoming instincts or emotions through the intellect. In the above circumstance the golfer must primarily make a conscious effort to apply dimension to a seemingly dimensionless situation. The fairway, especially on many opening holes, seems endless. The golfer must foreshorten it. He must define his goal honestly in terms of his capabilities. And he must gear his swing to those abilities, not to the power myth. This means that his goal must be some spot on the fairway well within his hitting capabilities. In short, he must accept reality.

Here is another interesting driving phenomenon: have you noticed that people who frequently drive erratically seem to lose balls more easily than good golfers who only occasionally hit bad shots? You would think that the consistently bad driver would actually be skillful in finding his ball, because he has more practice in doing so, but it doesn't seem to work that way. One reason for this is not that the ball is so difficult to find, but that the poor driver turns off his mind when he makes a bad shot.

This turning off a bad shot is an example of the defense mechanism of "denial." The golfer doesn't like what is happening, and, because he feels physically incapable of doing anything about the situation, his only recourse is to do something mentally. So he turns his mind off the ball; he denies its existence in the same way, perhaps, that he felt the ball denied *his* wishes. Consequently, his knowledge of where the ball finished is very often less accurate than that of the other players in his group who are only casually watching him swing. Also implicit in this experience is the desire not to find the ball at all, because its position might be so deplorable that the next shot would be unplayable. It is humiliating enough to have already hit one bad shot. Going on now to an impossible or embarrassing lie would add further insult to already serious injury.

By a conscious effort of will, this golfer must force himself to be objective about his shots. He must force

himself to watch the course of the ball no matter where
it might go, and accept the challenge of both finding
and playing it again, because objectivity is very, very
important in golf. If we allow our wishes to contaminate our sense of objective reality, we're going to
have to pay the price—both the mental price of constant
humiliation and negativism, and the actual cash price
of a lot of golf balls.

THE FAIRWAY WOOD SHOT

THE power myth carries over to the fairway
woods, but here there is a significant difference—the
golfer is no longer on center stage. He has already committed himself once on this particular hole, and, if the
drive was a good one, the green may now lie within
reach, making the need for restraint more acceptable.
Very few golf holes, except par-3s, are within range of
the tee for the weekend golfer, but on many par-4
holes, and even some par-5s, the green is well within
the reach of his fairway wood shots. Now the dimensions of infinity have been reduced to the realm of
possibility.

There are still some problems, however, the main
one being that the fairway wood shot must combine
distance *and* increased accuracy. The latter will come
hard if the power myth still lives.

There is also the fact that the fairway wood must be
played where it lies. This demands a versatility not
required on the tee, and the golfer unconsciously resents this fact: he has been spoiled by the luxury of
teeing the ball. Such resentment is often acted out in
the form of a tense, rushed, or jerky swing, inevitably
leading to a bad shot.

Fairway wood play, more than any other aspect of golf, makes dual demands. The shape and the feel of the club itself conjure up power images—teed-up balls, nonspecific distances—but the position of the ball brings the green into range and therefore demands greater precision in direction than is required off the tee. Many people find it difficult to make that mental adjustment. One golfer may swing the fairway wood powerfully but ignore the directional component. He'll hit long shots but will encounter many lost balls and unfavorable lies. Another golfer may find that he simply can't work out any kind of relationship with a fairway wood, in that he can't tee the ball as he does for a driver, nor bite into it as he would on an iron shot. This may cause him to give up and use an iron where he really should be using a wood. Yet another golfer may become so accuracy-conscious that he tries to "steer" the ball to the target instead of freely swinging the club. A loss of distance, and even accuracy, too, may result.

The answer to all these problems lies in understanding the compromise necessary between distance and precision with the fairway woods, and then accepting it.

THE LONG-IRON SHOTS

MOST pros will tell you that the long irons are the most difficult clubs to use, but what they rarely explain is that the reasons for this are not always physical. The mental difficulty again arises from the feeling that the long iron demands an involvement with two elements—distance and accuracy—but that in many ways this amalgamation is even more difficult here than with the fairway wood.

Few people have difficulty in accepting the concept of accuracy with an iron. Where the psychic problems arise with the long iron is in the area of power. The long-iron head is smaller, lighter, more knife-like than the bludgeon-shaped wood, and in this respect it does not seem credible that it can bang the ball a long distance. Because of this underlying doubt as to the long iron's capacities, there is often an unconscious attempt to beef up the swing with extra power. Again, this power comes from the large propulsive muscle groups, leading inevitably to a forced, ugly, jerky swing and a mis-hit shot.

Then there is the factor that the ideal long-iron swing is somewhat more down and through the ball, and less sweeping than the action required of the fairway wood. Many golfers find it difficult to adjust mentally to that physical variation.

The main psychological block in using the long iron is that people don't believe it can do what it is designed to do. That disbelief is reinforced by a fear of trying it. There is no magical solution to this fear. You've got to practice trying it. As the TV boys say, "Try it! You'll like it!" If you do, in time you'll begin to believe in it. To be an effective user of any golf club, "you've got to believe."

FROM THE ROUGH

THE shot out of the rough is uniquely traumatic in a number of ways. To begin with, the golfer generally approaches the ball with a psychic attitude of resentment, anger, or frustration. His stupidity has put him in this position where he has now got to face a less-than-ideal shot. And over there is his opponent, with his ball resting serenely in the middle of the fairway, giving him an easy shot at the green.

A cloud of negativism often settles over the golfer's mind at this point. Most of all he wants to get out of this uncomfortable situation. It's like a bad dream, to be erased from the memory as fast as possible. He is thus prepared to do anything that will simply end the agony. So, instead of giving the shot the extra time and creative thinking it needs, the golfer tends to make a quick assessment, a fast decision, and an even faster swing. We all know the result. . . .

Shots out of the rough call for more imagination, more creativity, and more mental control than most other shots in golf. It is these qualities—much more than his strength—that make Nicklaus so good at such shots. The very best golfers recognize this. The greatest professionals play shots from the rough with tremendous and clearly visible respect, making some of their finest strokes in some of the most difficult of golfing situations. The consistent tournament winner looks upon the "trouble" shot as a challenge, as one of the most exciting aspects of golf, whereas the average golfer sees a shot from the rough as a punishment—the just deserts of stupidity. This difference in mental approach is a major factor behind the difference in execution.

THE PITCH

BECAUSE the power myth is diminished here, most golfers find pitch shots less troublesome than most other shots. If you're only 100 yards or so from the green, it's easier to accept that you don't need to power the ball. What is needed is ball control, and since an iron appears and feels acceptable as a tool for this purpose, it's fairly easy to focus on precision alone.

But here we can run into Superego trouble, in that the focus on precision can sometimes become *too* sharp. You'll remember that the Superego demands pinpoint precision; it is interested only in absolute perfection. If there is one time on the golf course where the body has to be tension-free, it's in playing the short precision shots. When the Superego gets the upper hand, however, the intensity of the desire for exactness can become so great in some golfers that it can cause the hitting muscles to tighten, thus removing any hope of a smooth, relaxed, integrated swing. The tendency to look up is also obviously greater in this situation; indeed, the temptation to see where the ball is going can be almost irresistible to the Superego-controlled golfer.

Ball fixation can be another problem in pitching. The shortness of the shot brings us into a more intimate relationship with the ball, both physically by virtue of the shorter length of the club and psychologically because of the shorter distance to the target. This physical and mental intimacy causes us to focus more intently on the ball, which introduces the hypnotic forces we have discussed previously—often with the ultimate result of some kind of swing laxness, usually in the area of tempo.

Finally, we also have to deal with the common prejudice that a short shot, by virtue of its shortness, is an easier one. This can be a real danger, in that along with that prejudice goes a subtle lack of respect for the shot, a feeling that it really isn't as important as the longer shots. That kind of attitude destroys any hope the golfer might have of becoming an expert in this extremely important part of the game.

THE CHIP

CHIPPING intensifies all the factors we've mentioned relative to pitch shots. Here is an even shorter shot, and therefore one that inspires an even greater desire for perfection, or even less respect, or an even more hypnotic ball fixation.

Here there is a further complication, in that all the small muscles of the hands are on the alert. This is their kind of situation and they want all the action—and we are only too aware of what can happen to the club face when the hands do take total control. The chip shot also encourages the golfer's head to go forward or backward and from side to side. These are unconscious, imperceptible movements that force the swing off the proper track.

Chipping can also cause the golfer to experience what a friend of mine describes as a "chilly-dip." The shot seems so easy that he forgets everything that he has ever learned about golf, and as a result his mind goes into a mental paralysis that results in a total mis-hit.

THE SAND SHOT

FOR many people, the shot from sand can be the most traumatic in golf.

The texture of the sand itself promotes all kinds of

vivid imagery. Golf-course grass is like a lovely thick carpet, full of color and life. It invites positive attitudes. But sand is dead, dry, arid. Grass tends to be cushiony so the ball can set atop it. Sand tends to grasp and swallow the ball. There is something uniquely disheartening about the sight of a golf ball firmly settled in its little crater of sand. It is almost as if it were saying, "I am comfortably settled here and you cannot possibly get me out," or, at best, "You can get me out, but that's about all you can do. Don't expect me to go to any specific place."

I know golfers who have actually had nightmares about being in bunkers, in which the unconscious creative forces in their minds conjure up episodes of unparalleled agony. For example, the sand becomes quicksand, and their sleeping minds are filled with horror as they feel themselves sinking down under the inexorable force of the whirlpool that lies below them. This nocturnal fantasy is actually an expression of the kind of unconscious—sometimes even conscious—terror the unhappy golfer feels as his feet sink into the shifting sand of a real bunker.

The terror of bunkers felt by most golfers is so universal that it is almost perverted *not* to be afraid of the sand shot. And the psychological significance of sand is so great that all course architects rely upon it as one of their most powerful weapons against low scores. Many a fine round of golf has been spoiled because just one shot dropped into sand, and the mental effects of this experience can become so great that they build a deep and irrational fear of sand.

This fear is reflected by the fact that sand shots are one of the most neglected areas of golf in terms of practice. The reason is that most golfers deal with the problem by using the mental mechanism of denial. In short, they try to ignore it, to imagine it doesn't exist, in the hopes that it will never beset them. Their silent prayer is that they will play well enough not to have to face this dreaded problem.

In actuality, as any good golfer will tell you, the sand shot is one of the easiest in the game, once you understand its simple but special techniques and have experienced success with it a few times. The only way to eliminate fear of bunkers is to learn these techniques and then practice them. By simply ignoring or neglecting the problem, you ensure that it will haunt you like a ghost as long as you play golf.

PUTTING

PUTTING is the greatest psychological arena on the golf course, and many are the mighty who have fallen there.

In putting, the power myth is extinct. As hard as he may try, there is no way the golfer can benefit from any strength he may possess in this particular situation. For the big-hitter type, the very heart has been torn out of his game. The powerful muscles of the body must give way to a delicate—almost dainty—touch, which is enough to turn the stomach of any real he-man. Here he is, Superman, suddenly called upon to perform an act that any little old lady can equal. That is tough medicine to take for a certain type of psyche.

To many golfers, there is also the problem of a certain element of injustice in putting. Why shouldn't that puny little 5-yard putt be worth, say, only one quarter of the value of a 250-yard drive? After all, you don't have to be Einstein to appreciate the fact that the drive is fifty times longer than the putt. The fact that this kind of quantitative discrepancy is taken into account in most other games, but not in golf, is just another factor in the psychological maze that the golfer has to deal with when he walks onto the green.

The answer, of course, lies in overcoming this prejudice and giving to the seemingly simple and humble process of putting the same respect that is given to driving or hitting long irons. Unless a golfer can learn to respect and meet the formidable psychological implications of this situation, he will never reach the level of humility necessary to become a good putter, and therefore a good golfer.

The tremendous precision that putting demands is perhaps the most devastating mental problem most golfers have to face beyond the extinction of the power myth. While on most golf shots the course of the ball, from the time it is struck until the time it comes to rest, is influenced only by currents of air, the ball rolling on the surface of a green obviously is affected tremendously by the direction of the grain of the grass, the topography of the green, and the velocity at which it travels. In short, there are many more variables in putting than are imposed by the action of wind upon the ball. Thus, to become a good player, the golfer must learn not only to stroke the ball but to read the greens very accurately. This takes serious study and a great deal of experience, but most of all it takes *respect*— intellectual and emotional acceptance of the fact that putting is just as important as driving or any other shot.

Even when he has learned how to read greens—and has accepted the fact that there are too many variables for him ever to always read them perfectly—the golfer still has another problem in putting. This is that the putting stroke itself is a fallible instrument.

The most natural way for the golfer to roll the ball into the hole with the greatest amount of accuracy is to place the face of the club squarely behind the ball and simply roll it toward the hole. And that, of course, is exactly what he tries to do. But the degree of precision necessary to achieve perfection in that act is also beyond human attainment—mechanically and mentally. Mechanically, minute deviations of the club face or stroking path must occur from putt to putt. Mentally, some degree of tension must result from the worrying fact that when putting one is playing one's "last chance" shot.

So, even though the actual mechanics of the stroke may seem simple, its effective execution requires more mental control than that of any other shot on the golf course.

Indeed, no area in any other sport combines the need for courage, knowledge, confidence, precision, and humility to the same degree as the putting situation in golf.

The answer to all these demands lies, at root, in genuine mental *respect* for the part putting plays in golf. Given that, all the above qualities can be attained through practice and experience. Without it, they never will be.

5
Golfing Enemy
Number One—Anxiety

W E'VE all seen it happen. It's the seventy-second hole of a grueling, four-day tournament. Two men are tied for first place. Both are on the green of the par-4 eighteenth in two. After meticulous preparation, the first golfer strokes his putt, a twenty-footer. It misses by a hair.

The second golfer has only a three-foot putt for victory. It's a straight-in putt; there should be no problems. Some friendly foursomes would call it a "gimme." The tournament seems to be all over. But in the minds of every one of the millions watching the spectacle on TV, there rests the thought that this ridiculously short putt just might be missed. They hold their collective breath as the golfer swings his putter back. The electronic eye of the television camera follows the ball as it rolls to the hole and then slithers weakly by the right side of the cup. A groan goes up from the thousands of live spectators encircling the green. An even greater chorus of agonized cries arises from the millions of invisible spectators watching on TV.

What happened? Why did this man, who has held himself in total control for four days, fail on what appeared to be his last and easiest stroke? How is it that this brave, talented, highly trained athlete failed to do something that your grandmother could do nine times out of ten with her eyes closed and one hand behind her back?

Well, we can remove the physical element immediately. The golfer definitely knows how to putt in physical terms and had proved his ability at doing so for almost four days. The cause of this embarrassing and paradoxical failure must therefore lie somewhere else, and obviously that place is within his mind. His mind gave birth to a negative force. That force is "anxiety." It is Public Enemy Number One on every golf course in the world.

What is anxiety? It is a heightened sensitivity to physical and psychological stimuli that produces within a person a general sense of uneasiness. In one form anxiety can convert a beautiful physical movement into an action so uncoordinated as to be embarrassing to behold; and a clear-thinking mind into babbling idiocy. However, in another form, it can drive an ordinary person to superhuman effort and achievement.

The man who first linked this strange feeling with the activity of the adrenal glands was Professor Walter B. Cannon, of Harvard Medical School. He was able to demonstrate that anxiety was associated with an increased secretion of adrenalin into the bloodstream. But the intriguing question has always been whether a person becomes anxious *because* of increased adrenalin, or whether the increased adrenalin is due to some prior psychological event that *caused* anxiety, which then stimulated the adrenal glands. In other words, it's the old case of which came first, the chicken or the egg.

Either way, the fact remains that anxiety is both chemical and psychological. But, remember, it's the psychological—not the chemical—experience that bothers human beings. If man had no mind, the chemical constitution of his bloodstream couldn't have any effect on his sense of well-being.

Anxiety is a reaction to a situation, real or imaginary, that mobilizes man to one of two courses: "fight or flight." In terms of golf, it is the "flight" reaction that has such devastating effects upon the player. Although anxiety is the golfer's most serious mental problem, it's the one that most players tend to run away from, thus leaving themselves even more vulnerable to its effects than if they understood and accepted the problem. Most golfers give in to anxiety without a struggle, as though nothing could be done about it. This is not unusual, for men generally treat anxiety like the rain: they simply wait until it stops. But there *are* things that can be done about anxiety. No human being has to passively submit himself or herself to its whims.

Psychoanalysis deals with anxiety by going to the root of the problem that started it. Fortunately, in golf, most anxiety is not of such a deep-rooted variety. The causes are not hidden by unconscious defense mechanisms but are usually clearly discernible. Thus the problem becomes much more easily solvable.

What the golfer has to basically accept is that anxiety is a *real* problem, and one that he must deal with *consciously*, just as he would practice his putting, driving, or wedge shots. He must learn to recognize its causes, and he must then take definite and positive steps to get rid of them.

THE ANXIETY OF IGNORANCE

ANXIETY on the golf course is probably most often based upon a sense of inadequacy. In very few games does the performer put himself on the spot so completely as in golf. The golfer can't blame anybody else for his mistakes. He plays before a silent, yet intimate, audience that closely observes—and criticizes —his every move. Fear of inadequacy leads human beings down many pathways, and in golf it can destroy any hope of ever being a good performer.

Ignorance is one of the commonest causes of a sense of inadequacy, which in turn creates anxiety. Thus ignorance about the golf swing can produce anxiety.

The golf swing is an unusual physical maneuver, but it is definitely something that can be intellectually understood and physically learned. And, even though a golfer may never swing his club in the "right" way, he can almost always build into his swing some form of compensation for its irregularities. In other words, even though he may never achieve "perfection," he can almost always achieve a decent level of competence.

When a golfer compensates successfully by instinct rather than understanding, even though he may have a bad-looking swing, he will generally score decently and thus feel little or no anxiety. But often this kind of swing breaks down under stress situations, because it is based purely on instinct rather than on solid understanding of the swing mechanism. Then the un-knowledgeable golfer becomes involved in a vicious circle. By moving from one compensatory change to another, he desperately seeks the magic move that will put it all together. Each new "secret" may last for a while, but under pressure uneasiness returns and off he must go looking for yet another panacea.

A golfer who suffers from this kind of anxiety can be immensely helped by professional instruction, and by diligent practice of the principles he is taught. There *is* a right way to swing a club, and when the golfer learns it, the anxiety of ignorance is greatly minimized.

THE ANXIETY OF COMPETITION

COMPETITIVE tension is another major cause of anxiety, but in this case there are positive as well as negative results.

The plus factor is the alertness that results from adrenal glands secreting adrenalin into the bloodstream to enable the body to produce a special effort. This is something that every successful athlete quickly learns to welcome, for, without it, the competitor can slip into a state of listlessness, and his performance can sink into apathy.

The negative side of competitive tension is that it can be symptomatic of an ego problem. Everybody wants to win, but winning means more to some people than to others. If a golfer uses the game as a means of boosting his ego, then the game itself becomes of secondary importance. The golfer is then using golf to find self-acceptance. The game becomes a means to an end instead of the end itself. When the primary goal of golf becomes inflation of the ego, then the ego is at center stage, making the golfer uncomfortably self-conscious, and thereby anxious.

From here the golfer is led into the process of comparison. If an opponent hits a long drive, it's a threat to his own physical prowess, and he wants to hit an even longer one. Even if on that particular hole he might be wiser to use a less powerful club, his primary need is to demonstrate his physical superiority, and this temptation wipes out any intelligent consideration of the tactics of the game.

The answer to this is to strive for an objectivity that excludes comparing particular elements of one's game with those of other players. As we shall keep emphasizing, the *real* competition is between the golfer and whoever designed the course. Every golfer must continually remind himself of that fact if he is to keep his game in perspective and thereby sustain an objective attitude to his performance.

It is to avoid the traps of competitive anxiety that even the greatest match-players have generally "played the course" rather than the man. When a golfer starts playing against another player, instead of the course, he risks becoming subjective and emotional. And all decisions in golf have to be made by the intellect, not by the emotions.

THE ANXIETY OF GAMBLING

GAMBLING unusually high stakes on golf can cause anxiety, especially in a person who is more emotional than intellectual about his game. In this situation, defeat affects the golfer not only emotionally, but in the pocket as well, adding insult to injury. Indeed, it is my view that a golfer who gets emotionally involved with gambling would become a far better player if he did not bet at all, simply because he would be free to approach the game more objectively. It is true that betting can keep some sloppy golfers from becoming careless, because nobody likes to throw money away. But actually worrying about bets can produce a lot of anxiety and frustration in an emotional type, and that is definitely going to hurt his game.

Before you gamble for high stakes, you should be sure that you can maintain the level of your game under the extra pressure you are engendering. One of Jack Nicklaus's great assets on the golf course is his ability to concentrate. Although Jack plays for enormous stakes, with so much hard cash riding on each shot, I know from discussing the matter with him that his mind is completely free of thoughts about financial implications as he stands over the ball. This has been true of almost all the great champions, because handling the situation any other way is bound to open a floodgate to anxiety. Nicklaus expresses the ideal approach perfectly when he says, "I concentrate on winning, knowing that if I win the financial considerations will take care of themselves."

THE ANXIETY OF FAILURE

GOLF must be approached positively, but a golfer must also be prepared for failure. Learning to accept setbacks is part of the reality of the game.

Most golfers react to failure with anger, a reflex response that afflicts at times even the most controlled of players.

The anxiety associated with a dismal shot is the anxiety of frustration and futility and, uncontrolled, it is a certain game-wrecker. In fact, people who are unwilling to accept the frailty of human nature are always going to have a hard time at golf, because there are very few activities in which human vulnerability is so openly displayed. Even excellent golfers shoot a hole in double figures because they cannot stem the molten lava of anger in response to one bad shot. The hard fact of the matter is that a man who is not ready to accept bad shots is not ready to play golf well.

THE ANXIETY OF SUCCESS

STRANGELY enough, a good shot can also produce anxiety, which brings us to the concept of the "threat of success."

You might wonder how success could possibly threaten anyone. Well, for one thing, success is highly unpredictable. A golfer always knows he can fail, but he is not so sure that he can always succeed, and predictability is greatly appealing to the human mind in whatever form it may appear. Also, as I pointed out earlier, once you have succeeded others expect you to succeed again, which is a very frightening proposition to a lot of people. Success may threaten a golfer's relationship with his friends. The winner becomes the King of the Mountain, and everyone wants to pull him down. Also, as we've noted, success can breed loneliness, in that no longer can the winner identify with the great mass of losers—or they with him.

For these reasons, impending success often becomes a threat, and as such a possible source of anxiety. Thus, if you are an ambitious golfer, you must be ready to emotionally accept the uncomfortable aspects of being a winner as well as the pleasures.

THE ANXIETY OF HAZARDS

HAZARDS on the golf course are a rich source of anxiety and tension. Bunkers precipitate anxiety in all but the most expert golfers, and water, with all its regressive implications, has a strange way of mobilizing tension in all golfers. Deep rough, woods, out-of-bounds markers, all symbolize the unconscious fears of the golfer about the vagaries of his shot-making accuracy.

There is no magic way of dealing with these overt threats. The golfer must learn to be objective and to accept them as part of the total golfing challenge. The obstacles on the course cannot be ignored, but neither can they be allowed to control one's emotions.

Positive action can be taken in regard to at least some of the hazards. It is said that Gene Sarazen occasionally aimed for bunkers deliberately, because he played some sand shots better than he did a very long putt. True or not, this points up the fact that one positive way to reduce the tension surrounding bunker shots is to learn to play them well. The same thing applies to anxiety about rough.

This approach does not, of course, apply to water and out-of-bounds markers. These are much more threatening, in that there is no way you can shoot from the middle of a duck pond or a nearby cornfield. Again, the answer is to *respect* the hazard, but not fear it to the point of letting it stimulate a stream of totally negative thinking. All obstacles are designed to mobilize fear, but the golfer must counter this by striving for a positive objectivity that puts them into a secondary role in his thinking. His mental planning should include only the fairway and the green, not the obstacles. Overreacting to obstacles changes the basic emphasis of the game. The theme should not be avoiding hazards, but getting the ball into the hole in the least number of strokes.

THE ANXIETY OF IMPATIENCE

BECAUSE time loses its chronological character and significance on the course, golfers must learn to wait. A player who tries to jump ahead of time is in for a lot of trouble.

This applies not only to the execution of the swing itself, but to the actual playing of the game. Most weekend golfers move too slowly up to the shot and then too fast over it, whereas the great professionals generally are extremely deliberate in all their shot-making actions. This indicates that the pros have successfully dealt with the anxieties associated with the impulse to leap ahead of time. They realize that they have only one swing at the ball, and that once it's made there is no turning back.

One problem of the high handicapper is that, although he may sense the need for deliberation, he doesn't have much to deliberate about. This, again, involves the problem of ignorance. When Jack Nicklaus stands over a putt for what seems to be an interminable length of time, he isn't just posing; he's

actually thinking about something to do with the putt
at hand. His total understanding of the game and his
skill at putting this knowledge into positive action
are the qualities that make Nicklaus a great golfer. He
understands the dimensions of time in relationship to
golf. He does not dawdle and waste time needlessly
between shots—as many weekend golfers do—but
then again he is never in a hurry. He plays with dis-
patch within a framework of controlled deliberateness.

THE ANXIETY OF EMOTIONAL REACTION
TO OTHERS

EMOTIONAL involvement with other players can
create anxiety. An opponent with an irritating personality—conceited, condescending, egocentric, rude
—tends to mobilize the anxiety of anger in many
golfers.

Emotional reaction to another player can be very
dangerous, in that it can totally divert the focus of the
golfer's attention from the main theme of the game. It
may be gratifying to beat an obnoxious opponent, but
this is not going to happen if your mind is so consumed
by that desire that you cannot apply it to playing the
shots that will win the game.

When a golfer meets such an opponent, two problems arise. One of them is the personality of the opponent that the golfer finds obnoxious. There is nothing
he can do about that. It's the other man's problem. The
second and greater problem is the one within the
golfer's mind that allows him to react subjectively to
this kind of person. He must learn to recognize this

feeling as a warning that the mental part of his game is in danger of diversion, and he must deal with the reaction immediately by exerting the maximum objectivity.

There is no way another person's failings can affect any golfer's game unless he allows them to do so.

THE ANXIETY OF DISTANCE

LONG holes are another great source of anxiety. Looking out from an elevated tee at what seems to be an endless vista, toward a flag too distant to be visible, immediately creates tension in the less skilled golfer, especially if he has never played the hole before.

The anxiety here is plainly created by a fear of physical inadequacy. Yet, in reality, there is little to fear, in that almost all par-5 holes can be reached in three shots by most golfers. The problem actually is not the sheer length of the hole, but the fact that the golfer wants so much distance on his first two shots that hardly any will be left for the third.

Now, a pro can think that way, because he has the skill to achieve that goal. But too often this kind of thinking results in catastrophe for the average golfer. Looking for that extra bit of power, his muscles begin to do strange things. Generally, instead of reaching the green in three, he's lucky to get there in five.

Whenever a golfer knows he's not going to reach the green with his first shot, his chief thought should be to drive the ball safely into the middle of the fairway, thereby giving himself the best chance to make a good second shot. And even if after a good second shot he still has to use a wood on the third shot, so what? There's nothing wrong with that. He can still reach the green in three.

Obviously, all long holes are threatening. But that isn't really the problem. The real problem is that golfers are like Walter Mitty. They harbor in their minds grandiose dreams of reaching every par-5 hole they encounter in two shots.

These are unrealistic fantasies, manifesting our old enemy the power myth, or man's constant dream of outreaching himself. Try to appreciate once again that the power myth really has nothing to do with the game of golf. Rather it has to do with a puny ego, which only reinforces its weakness by reaching for the unreachable.

Even at the highest level, golf is *not* primarily a demonstration of strength, but a game of accuracy. For example, the club golfer is not asked the length of his drives, but what handicap he plays from.

The *real* man in golf is the one who can score well, not the one who can hit the ball far.

THE ANXIETY OF THE ELEMENTS

ADVERSE weather conditions—especially wind —are another cause of anxiety-bred tension on the golf course.

Most golfers, for example, overreact to wind. Faced with a strong wind, they want to hit the ball as far as they do when there is no wind at all. In consequence, they unthinkingly try to build into their swing a means of increasing power, the result of which is usually a slice, a hook, or some other disaster. Most golfers fail to ever think through the fact that, even if they are successful in putting a little more power into the shot, it is not really going to affect the course of the ball very much in the face of a strong wind.

Wind cannot be ignored. The golfer must face the fact that it is going to do something to the ball. Then he should try to minimize that effect through his intellect rather than his emotions. One obvious answer is to use a longer club. There are others, but the basic solution is to accept reality and adopt a logical approach to the problem. For example, if a gale is blowing in your face on a long par-4, it is in reality no longer a par-4, but a par-5. Reality therefore demands that it be played as a par-5.

What may help above all in bad weather is simply to recognize that whatever is happening to you is happening to everyone else on the course. The key is not to allow yourself to regress to a caveman mentality to deal with problems that can generally be solved with some intelligent adjustments to your shot-making strategy.

OVERCOMING ANXIETY

THESE are but a few of the anxieties suffered on the golf course. The golfer should learn to recognize them, because they are as detrimental to his score as the physical hazards that beset him.

Dealing with these anxieties is a two-phase process. First, the golfer has to identify the particular variety of anxiety that is afflicting him, and, second, he has to learn to "let go" of it. Identifying the anxiety, and understanding its source, provides the ammunition to deal with it, in that the golfer is no longer dealing in the dark with an invisible force.

Most people don't realize that we have a lot more control over internal nervousness and tension than we think we do. There is a kind of psychic gravity that operates in all our lives. If I can think of my anxiety as a physical object that I'm holding in my hand, all I have to do is to let go of it. This psychological gravity takes away the psychic mass in the same way that terrestrial gravity takes away a physical object that you release from your hand. Anxiety hurts most people because they continue to cling to it as though it were a teddy bear.

The key to getting rid of anxiety lies in using one's imagination; in converting the anxiety into a physical metaphor. Think of the body as a receptacle filled with a psychic fluid representing the anxiety. Let this fluid drain out of the system, beginning at the top of the head and moving right down to the tips of the toes. Don't be in a hurry.

Once acquired, this technique takes only about fifteen seconds and produces some very impressive results. It has been used in hypnotic procedures all over the world for years, and it can reduce tension much faster than any tranquilizer. The more one practices it, the more effective it becomes in getting rid of tension and anxiety.

The man or woman who scores consistently well in golf is the one who can deal most effectively with the anxieties I've outlined. Golf is meant to be played for pleasure, but as long as the monkey of anxiety rides on the golfer's back, it is certain to create misery.

6

Your Mind and Your Ball

THE PROBLEMS

OBVIOUSLY, a golf ball of itself possesses no actual mental powers, but that tiny sphere lying quietly in the grass projects several disturbing thoughts to the average golfer's mind.

For one thing, the ball's pristine whiteness suggests a virginal innocence that tends to imply that the task of striking it is really quite simple. As anyone who has attempted to play the game is aware, there is great folly in accepting that implication. The problems inherent in propelling that innocent-looking ball with any sort of predictability have led many a man to total mental and physical despair.

Then again, the ball's very lack of color—its pure whiteness—is suggestive of an extreme form of passivity, placing the responsibility for what will happen to the ball totally in the hands of the golfer. Now, the fact is that man generally reacts badly to extreme

responsibility: he always feels better if there is somebody else with whom he can share the load. But, as we
have discussed elsewhere, the golfer is very much
alone—he cannot shuffle off any part of his responsibility.

Another disturbing feature of the golf ball is that
it doesn't move until the player moves it. The immobility of the ball actually amplifies the responsibility
already imparted by its appearance of innocence. If
only the ball would move a little of its own volition,
there would be more excuses when things go wrong,
as in tennis where the player can rationalize his lack
of success in terms of some unexpected bounce.

The ball at rest deprives golfers of such excuses,
and to some the game in this respect can seem almost
unjust. The message transmitted is: "How can this
task be so difficult? Why should anyone have to go
through a complicated series of physical maneuvers
to hit a ball that's not even moving?" This reaction
is, among other things, an expression of man's fundamental resistance to any form of discipline. Man nearly
always regards discipline as a form of tyranny, not
realizing that it is often the most direct route to real
freedom.

Also inherent in this attitude is a subtle form of arrogance—a trap into which many high-handicap players fall in their endless search for the one magic
"secret" that will finally pull the golf swing together,
that will make the game simple for them forever more.
The low-handicap player, generally speaking, has long
ago seen through this illusion of simplicity arising from
the immobility and innocence of the ball. He has a
humility about his game, based on acceptance of
reality, that frequently eludes the high handicapper.

The sense of injustice resulting from the innocence and immobility of the ball can also lead to anger. Unfortunately, human beings usually react to injustice with anger, regressing to infantile behavior patterns of violent and uncontrolled rage. Anger is one of the most difficult of all human emotions to deal with, and the golfer must always be on guard against it, for anytime he allows it to infiltrate his game he's courting real disaster.

Finally the ball's immobility can make concentrating on it difficult. A ball that moves readily captures our attention, but to stare at a motionless object takes a very high degree of deliberate concentration. (This is one reason why many golfers do not really "see" the ball as they swing.) One effect of this is to make the performer increasingly self-conscious the longer he fixates on the object, and that in turn tends to build feelings of uncertainty.

The smallness of the ball is yet another factor that has a disturbing effect upon the golfer's mind. A golf ball seems disproportionately small when compared with balls used in other games, and hence demands a greater precision of strike. We tell ourselves that, if it were the size of a tennis ball, surely we would hit fewer bad shots. It is that subtle, unspoken demand for precision inherent in the relative minuteness of the ball that leads to anxiety and, thereby, frustrates free-swinging.

The smallness of the ball also unconsciously activates the small, sensitive muscles of the hands that, through a lifetime of experience, have always dealt with the fine manipulations needed to move small objects. Moving a large object like a piano, for example, never activates the smaller muscles—such a task is always associated with the movements of the larger muscles of the body, those of the back, arms, and legs.

Thus in golf we again encounter a frustrating paradox. The golfer must learn to use his large muscles to do a precise job that would normally demand the activation of his smaller muscles. At some time in their development most golfers have had the experience of the hand muscles disastrously taking over as the club head approaches the point of contact with the ball. If the ball were larger, this tendency would be diminished. But the ball is *not* larger, so once again objectivity becomes essential in mentally controlling one's physical behavior.

Not only is the golf ball small, immobile, and innocent-looking, but it is also physically remote. The shaft of a golf club is longer than, for example, the handle of a tennis racket, so that when the golfer looks down at the tiny ball, it sometimes appears to be so far away as to be almost out of sight. It seems to be saying, "Bend over and take a better look at me, because if you don't you could miss me altogether." This message is appealing to the golfer because it seems logical to him in terms of his experience in other games. It also seems to resolve the ultimate terror lodged deep in his heart—the fear of missing the ball altogether. This couplet of ideas imperceptibly draws the golfer towards the ball, as if it were a powerful magnet, encouraging him to lean over toward it, to try unconsciously to reduce the distance between his eyes and the ball. No wonder our instructors must continually tell us to address the ball with backs erect in a military fashion, to prevent us from giving in to the tendency to disrupt our swing axis by hunching over the ball.

Yet another characteristic of the ball that disturbs

the golfer's mind is its extreme liveliness, which allows men like Nicklaus to propel it 300 yards or more, double the distance Hank Aaron can hit a baseball, which we also consider lively! The liveliness of the golf ball tempts that part of man's personality that is infatuated with power (and there is a part of *every* man's nature that is susceptible to fantasies of power). What is generally overlooked here is that a golf ball is *so very lively* that it will go far with only normal force applied to it.

Although the golfer learns through experience that propelling the golf ball successfully demands precision above all else, there is a more primitive part of his psyche that eternally demands the expression of raw power. Most of us have felt that warm surge of manliness that follows a drive hit ten yards farther than those of the rest of the foursome. It's an experience that asks to be repeated, and no one is immune from this urge. The message the tiny ball transmits is: "Crush! Smash! Annihilate!" Too often, the golfer's Ego breaks down and gives in to this almost irresistible summons from his Id.

Every golfer knows that if he hits the ball hard and straight there is a possibility he can land in the circle of the Gods, shooting pars and birdies and eagles. But hitting the ball hard and not very straight can plunge the average golfer into an inferno of aching muscles and mental misery. At that point, the uncertainty of the outcome of *any* shot, coupled with the temptation to still crush the ball, will tear the golfer's mind into tiny pieces if he cannot make himself confront the temptation as an objective problem.

The fact that a golf ball is a comparatively expensive item is yet another source of mental stress to some golfers. Hitting a bad shot is humiliating enough, but also losing or cutting a precious object in the process adds insult to injury. It's surprising how this disquieting thought creeps into even the wealthiest golfers' minds at some time or other, as clearly indicated by the millionaire who gets out an old ball on a water hole.

Other messages are transmitted to the golfer by the ball that are unrelated to its physical characteristics. Here the golf ball acts as a crystal ball. As the golfer stares into its depths, he slips into a light stage of hypnosis, opening his mind wide to suggestion.

The actual suggestions, of course, come from the golfer's mind itself and are usually reflections of anxiety. "Hit me!" is the clearest and most urgent message transmitted, and it comes through with disturbing force while the golfer is reviewing in his mind the moves that make up the golf swing. Now, it takes an appreciable amount of time for the golfer to go through the physical preparation and maneuvers that result in an effective swing of the club. But, as the message "Hit me!" gets louder and clearer, the golfer finds it less and less tolerable to go through the total sequence of thinking and moving required to bring the club head squarely into the ball. As the swing progresses, the inner voice shouts the message louder and louder: "Hit me! *Hit me!* HIT ME!" And so the golfer does just that, lurching and lunging at the ball in his need to satisfy that compulsion as quickly as possible. The result of surrender to this kind of hypnotic suggestion is continuing disaster, and it is familiar to all golfers at some time in their careers.

The actual cause of the disaster is not the message "Hit me!" but the golfer's interpretation of it as "Hurry up." Almost all high handicappers under the influence of this kind of hypnotic conditioning from the ball completely abandon the concept of tempo. The general result is a swing that resembles more the thrust of a beleaguered swordsman trying to fight his way out of an ambush than a golfing motion.

As the golfer stares steadily at the ball, it also seems to ask him, "Where am I going?" Too many golfers find it irresistible to answer this question prematurely, which is why so many of us lift our heads before we've made contact with the ball. Any duffer can swing at a leaf on the ground and never raise his head. He can do so because he knows the leaf isn't going anywhere—or at least anywhere that matters. But this is not the case when he swings at a golf ball. He knows that where the ball goes is vitally important, and he is so anxious to discover its destination that he almost involuntarily peeks down its anticipated flight path even before he has hit it. Of course, he can't see anything because nothing's happened—yet! By the time something does happen, it is generally so bad that he wishes he hadn't even bothered to look.

It might seem from all this that golf is not actually a fun game, but rather some sort of Machiavellian conspiracy to reduce a person's brains to mush and to push him over the edge of reason into an abyss of despair. If so, why not just admit the impossibility of golf and get involved with another game more compatible with man's basic nature? Many a person has given in to that perfectly understandable impulse and thrown the whole thing aside. Generally, they have done so because they have failed to recognize a basic fact about the game of golf, which is this: *overcoming the natural impulse to cop out, to quit, to give up, is part of what being a golfer is all about.*

Certainly the game is difficult and ·frustrating, and always will be. But it is in the surmounting of those unique difficulties and frustrations that enrichment lies. And that is why so few people who once get truly hooked on golf ever give it up.

THE SOLUTION

AT first this may sound like heresy, but to overcome the problems of the golf ball you must start by learning to *ignore* it. That doesn't mean that you must forget the ball altogether. What it does mean is that *you* must control the ball instead of letting the *ball* control you.

A lady I know has one of the sweetest golf swings I have ever seen. Talking about her swing one day, she inadvertently told me something that I think just about says it all. "Once I start back into my swing," she said, "*I can't see the ball.*" What she is really saying is that, once she begins her swing, she doesn't *worry* about the ball, the reason being that by then her mind is occupied with much more important thoughts.

The obvious question is: "Well, if the golfer doesn't look at the ball, what *does* he look at?" The fact is that the expert golfer doesn't really "*look at*" anything—he doesn't specifically focus his eyes on anything tangible during the swing. We'll go more fully into the details of what he *does* do with his mind and eyes in a following chapter, where we deal with the use of images in the swing.

But it is important at the present time for the golfer to understand a basic principle of mental functioning, which is that the mind can be *aware* of many things at one time but can actually *concentrate* on only one of them. Thus, if the golfer focuses his mind on the ball, he cannot focus it on anything else during the swing. The ball can be moved neither by staring at it nor by the body acting directly, without the club. What the golfer should thus more logically do is concentrate on something that his mind/body complex *can* relate to directly.

Now, we have all been told to the point of it becoming almost the Eleventh Commandment that the most important thing in golf, as in all other ball games, is to "keep your eye on the ball." In actuality, this *simply is not true.* As we have mentioned before, golf is full of paradoxes, and this is perhaps one of the most important.

Obviously, for golfers whose minds have been totally conditioned to look at the ball, it is not easy to suddenly start ignoring it. Actually, apart from all the instructional exhortation to do so, looking at the ball is an automatic reflex in most people. This means that it's an unconscious behavior pattern that undercuts all intellectual interference. Indeed, it is impossible to alter such a reflex response by any conscious act of the will. Our reflexes act too basically in the mind structure to be eliminated by any *negating* act of the will. We cannot force ourselves *not* to concentrate on the ball by simply *telling* ourselves not to do so.

Instead the action taken must be *intellectually positive*, by which I mean that the golfer must very deliberately focus his mind on something more directly connected to his body.

What should that point of focus be? The golfer swings the *club head*, not the ball, and everything that happens to the ball is a result of what happens to the club head. If the club face passes correctly through the ball, then the ball will go correctly toward the target. So achieving the correct alignment and motion of the club head as it passes through the ball is obviously the main purpose of the swing. And, if this is true, then the most productive point of mental focus obviously has to be not the ball but the *club head*.

The golfer's top action priority, therefore, should be an awareness of the club head at all times. Even when it passes out of his range of vision, he must be mentally aware of both its position and tempo of movement. Failure to make this the top mental priority allows the mind to become detached from the club head. The mind works at a speed faster than light, so that, when it becomes detached from the club head, it has a tendency to dart right back to the ball, with the arms and hands trying to follow suit. Unfortunately, they are no match for the incredible speed of the mind. Consequently, in their futile attempts to catch up with the mind, they begin to flail uncontrollably. The awareness of the club head is lost in the sudden refocusing on the ball. The face of the club may twist, and the direction of the path of the club head may be diverted. The result is yet another half-hit or off-line shot.

When, however, the golfer focuses his mind on the *club head*, and keeps it there, all his movements are synchronized. The club head and the mind work together. A myriad tiny muscle changes synchronize to fulfill the intended task of swinging the club head squarely through the ball.

Then, too, the golfer unconsciously creates an image of the correct course or path of the club head within the memory bank of his mind. This image of the ideal path eventually becomes so familiar that the golfer doesn't really need to think about it. He simply *feels* it and over a period of time builds that feeling into his

eflex system, so that the proper swing path seems
upremely "natural." Once he gets to this point, any
leviation from that track feels unnatural. This is
exactly how the majority of top professionals play the
game, even though they may not articulate it quite this
way.

The golfer's ideal total image should involve not only
a particular path of the club head, but also a particular
tempo of movement. While feeling the club head moving along a specific track, he should also strive to
embrace in that feeling an awareness of *accelerative
momentum*. This momentum should be such that it
reaches its peak very close to the point where the club
head passes into and through the ball.

Making the club head the primary focus of the
golfer's attention gives him the independence from the
hypnotic effect of the ball that is indispensable to a
healthy golf-thinking process. Failure to do so exposes
the mind to powerful hypnotic influences that can play
havoc with the best intentions of the most dedicated
golfer.

We have mentioned before that the immobility of
the golf ball creates a problem of concentration, in that
it is much easier to pay attention to a moving object
than to a stationary one. However, the ball's immobility
is not entirely a negative force, in that obviously the
ball isn't going to move until it is hit, which means that
the golfer doesn't have to concern himself about its
position. Indeed, once he has developed a vivid image
of the path of the club head, he should theoretically
be able to make perfect contact with the ball even
when blindfolded. And, indeed, all the great golf
teachers and many of the touring professionals can
easily do this, which proves that, whether they are
aware of it or not, all golfers have the capability of

almost obliterating the ball from their vision. The subtle paradox is that, although the good golfer seems to be gazing fixedly at the ball his mind is actually occupied with other things. Primarily, in my researches these other things prove to be the club head's position and the muscular feel and tempo of the swing.

I firmly believe that the infamous putting disaster known as the "yips" is a clear manifestation of a person being mesmerized by the ball. The ball, through its hypnotic effect, causes the muscles of the hands and arms to congeal and jerk in an unsightly spasm that destroys any chance of a decent stroke. If the golfer could sometime make himself mentally ignore the ball by concentrating instead entirely on the speed and direction of the putter's head, his "yipping" days would, I believe, quickly be over.

The golfer should give serious consideration to all these aspects of the ball's effect upon his mind. Once they are faced head-on, they lose their mysterious power. In golf as in other aspects of life, too much of our time is spent avoiding confrontation with problems that could be easily dealt with if we simply brought them into the open and faced them squarely.

One of the main priorities of the student golfer should be to pull away the shrouds of mystery that cover so many aspects of the game. Placing the ball in proper mental perspective—making it work for *you* instead of you working for *it*—is a prime starting point in so doing. This not only frees you from the hypnotic influence of the ball, but also allows your body and mind to function together to achieve the goal you should set for yourself on every golf swing—that of swinging the club head squarely through the ball with the proper amount of speed for the shot at hand.

7
Your Mind and Your Target

ALTHOUGH most golfers are probably not aware of it, there are *two* targets and *two* missiles to be considered on every golf shot.

The *primary* target is the spot on the fairway or green where the golfer wants the ball to land. However, in order to reach this with any degree of accuracy, he has to become involved with a secondary target, which is, of course, the ball itself. If he strikes the secondary target well, he has every right to expect equal success in achieving the primary target.

Now we come to the two missiles. First, in relation to the primary target, there is the ball. And then there is the missile associated with the secondary target (the ball), which is, of course, the club head. Let's now consider all this a little more closely.

YOUR PRIMARY TARGET

MOST games in which a missile is projected to a target require that the participant focus his eyes steadfastly on that target. For example, the dart thrower never takes his eyes off the precise point on the board that he seeks to hit. The same rule applies to most pitchers in baseball, and certainly to the passer in football. The golfer, however, not only *turns away* from his primary target, but also looks in another direction, not briefly but from the start almost to the finish of his stroking movement.

When we see this done in other games, it is either in jest or part of a feinting maneuver—looking in one direction, throwing in another. But the golfer doesn't look away from his target because he's trying to out-maneuver someone or because he feels like kidding around. He does so because it is *anatomically impossible* for him to hit the ball in any other way. If he had eyes in the side of his head it might be managed, but unfortunately he doesn't. (Here, of course, is another cause of "head up." Golfers, like most other human beings, don't like to face up to their physical limitations, so they try to compensate for this disadvantage by looking up quickly after they have hit the ball—sometimes even *before* they have hit it.)

Because he can look in only one direction at a time, the golfer must carefully retain in his mind the image of the primary target—the area of fairway or green he seeks to hit—while he looks elsewhere as he swings. And, because it must be the basis for all of his mental and physical moves, this target image *should be as*

*clearly present in his mind as is the bull's-eye in the
actual vision of the dart player.*

Poor players seem rarely to take the time to fix that
primary target image sharply in their minds, most
probably because it seems too remote from the more
immediate problem of trying to hit the secondary
target—the ball—solidly. It's a case of: "Why should
I get too involved with something a couple of hundred
yards away when my real problem is lying right here at
my feet?" As a preliminary to the swing, these players
may look one or more times in the *general* direction of
the target, but even these are usually only token
glances. In short, because poor golfers do not look
at anything specific, *no specific image of the primary
target forms in their minds.*

What these golfers fail to realize is that the estab-
lishment of the primary target image in the mind is
the cornerstone of all the activity—mental and physical—concerned with the propelling of a ball in a de-
sired direction. Once the golfer loses close mental
touch with his primary target, he's swinging freely in
the breeze, and where the ball will go is anybody's
guess.

We are often led to believe that the most important
ingredients of the golf swing are the ways in which
we grip the club, or address the ball, or move our hips
or shoulders. No one can deny the importance of these
conscious muscular moves. But let's for a moment suppose that the golf swing is accomplished by the movements of exactly sixty-four muscles. How many of
those movements do you really think are controlled
by the human will?

For example, let's assume that the straightening
of the left arm occurs in response to a deliberate act

of will, and also the torsion-like windup of the back
and shoulder muscles, and the sideward shifting of the
hips. And let's suppose this accounts for thirty-two
muscles activated by conscious will. That still leaves
thirty-two muscles unaccounted for. And if those muscles are not under the influence of the conscious mind,
then what directs them? The answer, of course, is the
unconscious mind.

It is the muscles that are under the influence of the
unconscious mind that respond to *images*. If these
muscles are not provided with a clear image, they will
move according to their own devices, which are often
not in accordance with the intentions of the golfer.
However, when these muscles *are* given a goal-oriented
image, there is an excellent chance that they will synchronize to achieve that goal.

That is why it is so vitally important for the golfer
to consciously select a *highly specific* primary target
and to retain that target image in his mind's eye
throughout his swing.

YOUR PRIMARY MISSILE

THERE is not much to be said about the primary
missile, the ball, in this phase of the golfer's thinking.
Ideally, he has a clear image of the ball's flight from its
location on the ground to the primary target, so the
primary missile is actually at this point part of an
"end" image—the projection of something that's going
to happen *after* the golfer has committed himself by
swinging.

Inclusion of the flight of the ball in the total image of

the target makes that image dynamic rather than static, which is helpful in preparing the golfer for action. Even more important, however, is a clear mental image of the ball being projected through the air and landing in the target area, because this above all reinforces the theme of success. If the golfer fails to form this image, he's allowing himself to think that he really can't do the job, which is the first breach in the dike that will permit an influx of negative thinking. And if ever negative thinking is allowed to flood the golfer's mind, he might as well give up the game and take up weeding the garden. So an image of the ball successfully reaching the primary target is as important as a clear picture of the primary target itself.

YOUR SECONDARY MISSILE

ALTHOUGH the golfer might agree with the logic of our previous argument that the ball is really the secondary target, it will probably still seem to him the most important functional target, in that it is the primary missile. But *should* it be?

Most golfers might think it superfluous to project a mental image of the club head's path in both the backswing and the downswing. Yet, because the margin for error is so narrow in golf, anything that will contribute to greater accuracy is vitally important. And what is more important than the club head in this respect? Here, in fact, is the *controlling* missile. It must be delivered squarely into the ball for the primary target to be achieved. And how is the golfer going to achieve this unless he thinks about the club head—unless he clearly imagines and pictures its path away from, and back to, and through the ball?

YOUR SECONDARY TARGET

WE have said that the secondary target is the ball itself, but in order to hit the bull's-eye the golfer should not really be "looking" at the ball mentally, but rather at *the image of the missile—the club head— as it should be when it strikes the ball correctly.* Even as he swings the club head back and out of sight, his mind should remain focused on the image of the club head in its ideal hitting position. Should the golfer instead allow his mind to shift from a picture of the club head's behavior at impact to the ball itself, he immediately opens up the Pandora's box of hypnotic influence described in the chapter "Your Mind and Your Ball."

In short, the ideal mental image in golf is *not* a clear impression of the ball, but rather *a picture of it being directed to a primary target, interrelated to a picture of the club-head path that will direct it there.*

I'm sure that many golfers will object to these ideas. The axiom "Keep your eye on the ball" is so ingrained into most people's minds that any deviation from it is likely to automatically be considered heresy.

If that is your reaction, then all I would ask you to do is to study a photographic swing sequence of any good golfer. There is no question that, as he begins his swing, he seems to fix his eyes on the ball as though mesmerized. Even when he is at the top of the swing, with all the muscles of his back and arms pulling at his head, his head remains steady, with his eyes apparently fixated by the ball. And even on the down-swing, when his lower body is shifting hard toward the target, the good golfer still appears to maintain that fixed gaze.

Then a very remarkable thing happens. Even after he has hit the ball, and the club and his hands and arms are well into the follow-through, the top golfer's head remains unmoved, as if still transfixed by the ball. But, of course, the ball is no longer there. Then what in the world is he staring at? What he's staring at is *the image of the club head that he produced when he placed it behind the ball in the process of setting up for the shot.* In short, he reached the climax of his swing when he brought the club head into that imagined position behind the ball, and he's still looking at it. Only as the momentum of the follow-through forces his head to swivel and his eyes to seek the result of the shot is this mental picture of the club head's behavior actually replaced by the image of the ball itself.

To achieve maximum control of the club-face alignment and acceleration, the golfer must in my view do three things simultaneously. One, he must have an image of his primary target implanted in his mind. Two, he must orient all of his physical movements around the imaginary arc and tempo of the club head, from the take-away, through contact, and into the follow-through. Three, he must continue to "look" at the image of the phantom club head into which he is going to swing the real club head precisely at the moment of contact. We'll talk about the details of these vitally important images when we discuss mental swing dynamics in the following section.

To end this chapter, let me stress again that the golfer must be very clear in his thinking about his

actual targets and missiles, and he must clearly understand their relationship to each other. Without such
understanding, the golfer is actually playing in the dark
as far as his mental functions are concerned.

8

Your Mind and Your Method

BEFORE THE SWING

THE first mental situation the golfer faces on every shot is what he *intends* to do with the ball. Obviously this decision requires the selection of a target and the formation of an image of a shot going to it.

I deliberately used the word "intends" rather than "wants" above, because there is a big difference between the two, and it pertains to reality. The golfer must honestly assess his own ability to meet the challenge at hand. For example, average golfers spoil more shots by underclubbing than for any other reason. The golf manuals may recommend a wedge at 110 yards, but if the golfer knows he can't hit a wedge more than 80 yards, he must listen to himself. If the shot needs a 7 iron, then the golfer must use the 7 iron. When the reckoning is done at the end of the game, no one will ask what club he used on a particular shot—it's the score that counts.

In the same way, the golfer must also accept the reality of the climatic and ground conditions at any given time. He must know the effect of wind on his ball and make appropriate allowances. He must be aware that on heavy, moist days he's not going to get as much distance as on hot, dry days; that if the ground is hard, the ball will get extra roll; that if it's wet and spongy, the ball may get little or no roll; that if the terrain slopes downward he must allow for extra yardage in his mental computer, and vice versa if it slopes upward.

The golfer, in planning each shot, must also know when to be cautious and when to be brave. Many fine players put themselves out of the running because they always try to take the hero's way—straight over water to the pin, for example, when they should have gone the safe way around the water, even though it might mean having to deal with a longer putt.

Once the golfer has defined his objective, based upon his own ability and all the external physical factors, he is ready to think about its implementation.

The golf swing is a physical move, usually learned by imitation. The student identifies with the professional, in a sense inviting his teacher to come into his body and make the moves until he can make them for himself. It's because imitation is so much easier for the younger person that he learns the golf swing faster than the older golfer. The young mind has not yet been conditioned by things learned in other games, or by other physical situations in life that might contaminate the pure, coordinated flow of a good golf swing.

The golf swing, then, is generally learned from external influences, but these are only part of the story. Although the swing is a series of learned movements the golfer has seen in others, it is also activated and integrated by thoughts and other mental maneuvers within his own mind. People rarely talk about this internal activity, yet everybody knows that it goes on. It's almost as if it were a tightly guarded secret. Whether he knows it or not, man uses imagery and thought hierarchies in ways that he cannot always express verbally.

One of the marks of a great golfer is the ability to concentrate. Just as surely, one mark of a poor golfer is the inability to concentrate. What makes the difference? Golfers who concentrate are golfers who are thinking about something *specific*. Conversely, the poor concentrators are those who think about nothing—or who try to think about so many things that they might just as well be thinking about nothing.

The golfer who concentrates goes through a very specific mental and physical checkoff system in preparing for and playing every shot. His approach to the swing is highly structured and organized. His mind doesn't leap ahead of his movements, because he knows what feeling or image to anticipate along each millisecond of the swing. He uses images deliberately and exchanges one image for another at the appropriate point in the sequence of actions that are required to play each shot.

The good golfer's mind is, therefore, not a vacuum, as some people would have you believe. It is very active, along a particular channel, and it remains on course because it knows where it's going. As we've mentioned before, the golfer is like a diver who stands at the foot of the board and carefully reviews in slow motion each action of his complicated gymnastic movement. When the diver's image is formed in exactly the way he desires, he rises up on his toes and duplicates physically what he has so carefully rehearsed mentally.

The golfer's contemplation as he addresses himself to his problem is, however, much more complicated than that of the diver or gymnast, or probably any other sportsman. The reason is that he has to deal not only with a very difficult and in many ways an "unnatural" physical maneuver in terms of his own body (the swing), but also with the extraordinarily difficult ballistical problem of bringing the comparatively small surface of the club very precisely into contact with a tiny ball at very high speed. What the golfer strives for in his swing is a repetitive sequence of muscular movements and feelings that will predictably do both jobs. The gymnast or diver, on the other hand, has only to consider the tempo and precision of his actual physical movements, and his action therefore can be, and is, more egocentric. The golfer is forced out of the egocentricity of his physical maneuver because the behavior of the ball is the ultimate determinant of how well he has performed. A beautiful swing that does not move the ball effectively is totally without value.

The preliminary procedures basic to playing any golf shot seem to be looked upon by many poor golfers as irrelevant. As far as they're concerned, they just want to stand up and hit the ball. All of this falderal about lining up the body parallel to the target line, and adopting a particular posture, and gripping the club in a very special way is "much ado about nothing." In most instances, this attitude is a reflection of the golfer's total ignorance of the complexity of the problem. It's a form of arrogance based upon ignorance.

It is not my mission here to advise anyone in the

specifics of how to take hold of a golf club and how to set up to a golf ball. Many golfers much more expert than I have been writing about these fundamental "statics" of the game for years. My point is simply that these steps are extremely important ones and must be so accepted mentally by any golfer seeking either improvement or greater consistency. Unimportant as they may seem when compared with the moment of truth —the hit—unless these "irrelevant" details are respected, the moment of truth will be a moment of despair. So don't neglect your "statics." If you do your homework in this department, it's going to be that much easier for you when you get into the action phase of the swing—the dynamics.

DURING THE SWING

BEFORE the golfer even gets to the ball, he is (or should be) already deeply involved in the formation of his target image. It is only around that image that he can create all his static and dynamic moves. Only after the target image has enabled the static requirements to be met—grip, alignment, posture, etc. —should the golfer become actively involved in the thoughts and images that motivate his actual swing.

The most important action image is the mental picture of the overall swing. To play well, a golfer must be very familiar with the *feel* of a proper swing, and to be able to feel a proper golf swing he must be very clear in his mind that this swing is different from any other motion he's ever made with any other kind of implement. For one thing, he must understand that the golf action is a swing *through* something, not *at* something. This is not an easy feel to learn either mentally or physically. The outstanding player/teacher Johnny Revolta once said that it takes about three years for anyone to get that feel. Nevertheless, however tough it is for him to develop, the golfer must continue to mentally retain that concept.

In my view, the most useful working image for the golfer to employ in terms of swing motion is that of the old-time slingshot, like the one David used against Goliath. The velocity of the stone in the slingshot is determined by the amount of centrifugal force that the slinger can impart to it. Now, this force does not come, as most novice golfers instinctively think it does, through the direct application of power through the contraction and extension of muscle groups. The weight lifter bench presses 300 pounds by applying the force of his contracted muscles directly to the weight. The golfer, however, achieves power through leverage, resulting from muscular contraction–extension. Using the left arm and the shaft of the club as if they were a sling, he derives his power from the rotation of shoulders and hips and the driving of the legs in the form, ultimately, of centrifugal force.

Thus, the golfer's job is to apply muscular moves synchronized into a smooth and powerful levering or *slinging action* of the club head. The shoving, pushing, grabbing, and heaving that we see so often are a clear regression to the more familiar ways of applying muscular force. In many instances, instead of his muscles doing what the golfer wants, the golfer does what his muscles force him to do. The problem here is, of course, that he is bound by ineffective muscle habits that go back many years. He can begin with the purest of intentions, visualizing the ideal swing motion very clearly, but, if the image is not indelibly embedded in his mind, he may lose it as soon as he sets his club in motion. His muscles begin to extend and contract; his hands and arms get overactive; and what is visualized as a precision slinging-type swing becomes, in effect, an axe blow.

It might be helpful to consider the sling image in a little more detail.

From the point of view of the external observer, the most prominent anatomical contributor to the golf swing is the sweeping action of a rod-like left arm rising up to a more or less vertical position above the head and sweeping down again through the ball. This action predominates visually in that the club is directly attached to the arms through the hands, and the arms and hands move through a much greater distance than any other part of the anatomy during the swing.

We have mentioned before that golf is a game of paradoxes, and none is more striking than the one I have just mentioned. For, although the arms—especially the left arm—seem to be the most important contributor to the power of the golf swing, they are in most good players essentially passive, acting simply as the outer end of the sling or lever. The main power of the modern golf swing actually comes from the muscles of the legs and back, operating in much the same way as a coil spring.

It is very difficult for the novice or untrained golfer to make himself believe this mentally and thus to assimilate it physically. As a result, many golfers meet their Waterloo simply by being overactive with their hands and/or arms in relation to their back and leg muscles. Psychologically, if a golfer moves his hands and arms back too actively, or speedily, it will make him very aware of his hands and arms, and the more aware he is of these limbs, the less aware he becomes of the large muscles in the back and shoulders that really should be supplying the power for his shots. Indeed, one reason so many golfers underpower their shot is because they in effect swing the club *only* with their hands and arms, either not using their backs and legs at all, or to such a limited degree that they are ineffectual.

We are not going to get any farther into physical swing technique here, except to suggest that in all his practice the main muscular focus of the golfer's mind should be on those big muscles that will give his swing power—such moves as the full backswing shoulder turn and, coming down, the lateral slide-and-turn of the hips and legs toward the target that is so predominant a feature of the top professionals' swings. When the golfer focuses his mind on these muscles, not only does he bring them more completely into play, but also automatically slows his tempo to synchronize with the more ponderous moves of the larger muscle groups. When he takes his muscular clues from his hands and arms, then frequently his tempo will get ahead of the club head and leave the big muscles—and their power—either far behind or out of play altogether.

In short, even though the golf swing demands an extraordinary degree of precision, it is most easily and effectively accomplished *without* the manipulation of the smaller muscles—yet another of golf's paradoxes. Unfortunately, the temptation to use the smaller muscles—especially those of the hands—at some time during the swing is one of the golfer's biggest mental battles.

Now let's look at the "mental dynamics" of golf in a little more detail.

GETTING STARTED

HAVING formed his primary target image and blended it with the secondary target image (the ball), ideally the golfer can now begin to relate both to an image of the swing required and to the pattern of impact it must achieve to meet his target goals.

Once he is satisfied with the target image he has formed in his mind—and this may take several looks between the target and the ball—he places the club gently behind the ball and focuses his attention on the top of the club head. Here he must form the image of the club head very carefully in his mind, because it is into this phantom image that he is going to swing the real club head on its journey *through* the ball.

Once the best golfers feel mentally ready to begin the swing, the majority of them press gently forward on the club shaft in a move analogous to the diver rising on his toes before he dances off the board. I think one reason the forward press is so popular is that it symbolically releases any residual tension that the golfer may have in his system.

GOING BACK

AS he begins to swing the club head back, the biggest temptation the average golfer must fight mentally is that of his hands becoming overactive.

One common cause of this is an almost imperceptible squeezing of the fingers as the club starts back. Apart from any physical manipulation of the club face this motion may cause, it brings an awareness of the hands a little closer to the golfer's conscious mind. Whenever that happens, there is a danger that the hands and arms will be brought into an active power role, thereby blocking out the golfer's awareness of the back and leg muscles that really produce power. And I repeat again that the importance of the golfer's awareness of the actions of these large muscles can never be overemphasized. They're his true source of power, and he must be mentally conscious of that fact if he is to tap that power to its fullest potential.

The club head weighs very little. The shaft weighs hardly anything at all. Yet how many times have you seen golfers lift the club as if it weighed three tons? They do so because they have been deceived into thinking that the left arm is the golfer's power source. The principal functions of the left arm are to position the club at the top of the swing so that maximum velocity can be transferred to the club head as it descends into and through the ball, while returning the club head to its square address position. It should be understood that these are both *control* functions and have nothing to do directly with power.

The overall tempo of the swing must be synchronized by the movements of the large muscles, which again is a difficult problem in mental discipline, especially if the unwary golfer allows his mind to receive from the ball the message: "The heck with everything else! Hurry up and hit me!" The golfer may keep his eyes on the ball, but he must keep his mind focused on the image of the phantom club head that he formed during the "getting started" phase. He must remember that the climax of his swing occurs as he brings the real club head into the phantom one, and not before.

I have emphasized that the primary function of the left hand and arm is to stabilize the club's alignment throughout the swing. To achieve such control takes physical as well as mental practice. If not carefully guided up into an optimal position, the left arm can gradually wander off in strange directions, requiring complex compensations at some other point in the action. In actuality, such small adjustments—which many of the top players make—usually happen at an unconscious level, and the golfer is not aware of them. However, like all compensatory moves, they are best avoided, both physically and mentally.

AT THE TOP

THE position at the top of the swing is very crucial. All the preliminary strategy has been carried out. All the muscular movements to this point have been away from the ball. Now the golfer stands at the threshold of actual commitment. In a few milliseconds he must measure the effectiveness of all that he has done.

It's very interesting that quite a number of golfers get "stuck" at the top of their swings. This psychological locking is a manifestation of the golfer's fear of the consequences of his commitment. It's like two guys arguing in a street brawl. The two opponents stand shouting increasingly vehement obscenities at one another, each waiting for the other to throw the first punch. This kind of arguing can go on forever, in that both assailants are afraid to make the first move, because once it's made there is no turning back. So it is with the golfer who knows that, once he leaves his position at the top, that's it—the ball is going *somewhere*.

It's the fear of the consequences of actually hitting the ball that can really paralyze a certain type of golfer and that creates such destructive muscular tension in so many others.

Such problems are compounded by the fact that it is also at this position that the club head—and the golfer psychologically—is farthest away from the ball. And it is also the point at which it is most tempting to become hypnotized by the ball, in response to the loud and clear message: "*Look* at me! I'm so small that if you don't you're gonna miss me." The demand of the ball for mental fixation at this stage of the game has an undeniable appeal. But if the golfer gives in to it, he will lose the phantom image of the club head that he so carefully formed when he began the swing.

COMING DOWN

AS any pro will tell you, if you've done everything right up until now the downswing is easy. All you have to do is let it happen. You've wound up the spring. All you have to do now is release the safety catch and see how well it works. This is a great attitude, and one the golfer should cultivate. But it is never easy to maintain, because the temptations coming down are many and powerful.

Ideally, the golfer starts his downswing turn with a slight lateral shifting of his lower body—the driving legs that unwind the power of his pivot into the ball. This seems to have to be a mentally deliberate move for most average players, because otherwise they will do what comes naturally, which is to hit from the top with the hands and shoulders—the arms and hands trying to take over not only the direction of the club, but also the generation of power. Thus it cannot be repeated enough that, in the modern golf swing, the prime role of the arms and hands is that of *directing* the club and *transmitting*, rather than generating, power. Mentally, one must accept the fact that power is generated by the bigger muscles, the hands and arms being related to it like the wire through which electricity runs. They are simply the conduit through which the power passes to the club head.

The downswings of the majority of poor golfers are made in a spirit of frenzy. They seem to be in an extreme hurry to hit the ball with their hands. But the golfer must *never* be in a hurry with his hands as he starts the downswing. It is the one time when he has to do what human beings find so difficult to do in any circumstances, which is to *wait*—wait until the hands are automatically activated by the lower-body action.

The downswings of many great pros often appear "lazy." You can see this particularly in watching a man like Jim Dent, who presently is believed to hit the ball longer than anybody on tour. His hands do not appear to be in any hurry at all to get the club head down into the ball. The reason his moves look so easy is because we are looking at his arms, and in the process overlooking the real source of his power, his back and leg muscles.

AT IMPACT

MANY golfers quit at impact. One of the main reasons they do so is that they have not grasped a fundamental principle of the swing, which is that the golfer must swing the club head *through*, not simply *to*, the ball. For people who have been throwing objects *at* things all their lives—as in baseball or football—there is an enormous mental obstacle to overcome here. But the golfer is going to face misery until he does overcome it.

The principle of swinging *through* the ball involves almost ignoring the ball, because, if you're truly going to swing *through* something, you're going to have to swing as if it were *not even there*. We've discussed this problem previously in talking about the role of the ball, but the basic fact bears repeating. Mentally, the golfer should picture bringing the actual club head down and into the phantom image of the club head as it rested behind the ball prior to the initiation of the swing. Reproducing the phantom image of the club head with the real club head is, then, the entire objective of the swing. All the ball does is lie in the path of the real club head as it reproduces the phantom club head.

At impact most golfers immediately raise their heads. It seems as though impact is a physical signal that releases them from the task of keeping their heads in a fixed position. Here again is a critical difference in the mental imagery of the good and the poor golfer. The good player continues to stare at the ground following impact, because his primary follow-through image is of the club head path and alignment. Only when his head is forced to swivel by the momentum of the club head is this mental image replaced by the flight of the ball.

FINISHING

A golfer can't help finishing well if he has done everything else well. But the image of the well-balanced follow-through must be part of the total image that he forms in his mind in preparing for the shot—it *must* be part of the total image of the golf maneuver. Some people think mentally picturing the follow-through is like locking the door after the horse has been stolen, in that the ball is already well on its way. But to leave this component of the swing out of the total image is, psychologically, a serious sin of omission, in that if there is no picture of the follow-through as part of the overall swing image, it is impossible to swing freely *through*, rather than *to*, the ball.

9

Using Your Mind to Teach
Your Muscles

I have repeatedly emphasized that the golf swing is a complicated physical maneuver, and that one of the reasons for this is that its execution involves the containment of deeply ingrained reflex responses developed through other activities. If, as all the great players and teachers maintain, the golf swing involves hitting *through*, rather than *at* or *to*, the ball, then—because the mind can concentrate only on one thing at a time—the golfer must mentally become fully involved with the club head. This means to all intents and purposes that he must only be *aware* of, not *fixated* by, the ball.

But *how* can you ignore something that's staring you right in the eye? That's the big question. And it's one of the toughest mental chores to accomplish.

FOCUSING ON THE CLUB HEAD

AS I've said, the first thing the golfer must do is make the club head his primary action focus point. This is the thing that he slings. If he slings it accurately, the ball flies straight and true. If he slings it imperfectly, the ball will not fly as he desires. The golfer must accept this as an intellectual truth and remind himself of it continually, so that it becomes etched in his thinking. He must reinforce it in every way possible, for example by deliberately focusing his mind on the club head as he sets up, positioning it exactly as he wants it to go through the ball, and waggling the club to get the feel of its weight in his hands.

The practice swing of the average duffer illustrates the importance of thinking club head rather than ball. Without a ball his swing is as free and fluid as any you will see on a golf course, because his mind is not on the ball. But when the ball is introduced, it's a different proposition. The mind has a tendency to short-circuit immediately to the ball, and this will always happen unless other feelings are produced to counteract it. When the mind switches to the ball, it carries the muscles along with it, and hitting *through* is replaced by hitting *at*.

In this respect, I suggest that one of the most important exercises to develop consciousness of the club head is to swing the club without a ball in sight: to first develop a swing and *then* superimpose it upon a ball. As a special exercise, I would even recommend swinging the club head wearing a blindfold. This exercise, better than anything I know, forces the mind to become aware of the muscular moves that comprise the golf swing.

Minds are easily distracted. When the golfer prepares to swing a club with his eyes open, the primary focal point of his attention is the ball. Then, when he starts to swing, his muscles cause his mind to "see" the motion of the club. Immediately, he is in an ambivalent situation. Part of him wants to watch the ball, while another part can't help noticing, and becoming partially involved in, the movement of the club head. Ambivalence in human experience always leads to conflict, which causes lack of concentration. This leads to confusion, which is then passed on to the muscular system. Result: the swing loses rhythm and symmetry.

The golfer who routinely allows his mind to focus fully on the feel of the club head and the muscles that sling it by swinging with his eyes closed is establishing a muscle awareness that will remain after he has opened his eyes and is actually swinging through a real golf ball. The same stimuli that diverted his attention before he programmed the muscular pattern will still be there, but the pattern will eventually become so deeply impressed into his system that his mind can ignore the diversion.

The golfer must picture most clearly in his mind the *image* of the club head as it swings through the ball. In the formation of this image he must try to include all the factors that influence the flight of the ball: the path of the club head, its velocity, its angle of approach, and the angle of the face as it relates to the distant target. This image of the club head's ideal behavior *is the most important functional image the golfer can form*, because it is the one that will determine the behavior of the club head at the point of contact, which, in the final analysis, is the only point that matters.

DRAINING AWAY TENSION

I have mentioned before that the golf swing is really a "sling." The power of the sling is very closely related to the amount of leverage the slinger is able to build up in his back and leg muscles during the backswing, and then release via a recoil action during the downswing. The power of both the coiling and recoiling actions is related to the optimal stretching of the muscles employed, and this optimal stretching can occur only in muscles that are relaxed. It is, therefore, imperative that, before every shot, the golfer drain every last drop of tension out of his system.

Freeing the muscles of tension should be an important part of every practice session, because the more the golfer practices tension drainage, the easier it becomes for him to do so under competitive conditions, where tension has a tendency to continually build up.

Physical tension—a feeling of stiffness or uncoordination in the muscles—is the result of a general contraction in many muscle groups of the body. It makes the golfer feel awkward, all his moves becoming disjointed maneuvers with little or no smooth muscular flow.

The golfer cannot get rid of tension by taking tranquilizers, or other forms of medication, because the side effects would destroy the physical execution of the game and perhaps also seriously distort his mental

functioning. The only certain way the golfer can overcome his situation is by the use of the imagination.

Begin by thinking of your body as a receptacle con-
taining liquid tension. The tension is distributed
equally within and throughout your body. Now close
your eyes and take a deep breath. As you inhale that
breath, begin to feel the receptacle empty from the top
to the bottom. Feel the liquid tension passing down
through your forehead. As it does so, feel the muscles
in that area relaxing, and, as they relax, the skin of the
forehead becoming smooth. Now the fluid, flowing
warmly, continues to move down, through the eyelids
and on into the lower part of the face, and then on
down through the neck and shoulders and into the
arms. A tingling sensation in the hands confirms that
all of the tension has left the arms. A slumping of the
shoulders indicates that the tension is now draining
out of that area. Now the fluid flows down through the
chest and abdomen, then out through the hips and
down and through the legs. Eventually you feel it passing through your ankles into, and out of, your feet. A
tingling of the toes signals the fact that the body is now
free and empty of tension.

With your eyes still closed, concentrate your attention upon this tension-free feeling and associate with
it the word "calm." Register this word very firmly in
your mind, for it signifies the feeling you want throughout all of your game. Program your mind, then, to
remember this feeling. Wear it like a coat. Try to cover
every move you make in relationship to the ball with
that feeling. Once the feeling is indelibly recorded in
your mind through practice, you can immediately
acquire it by use of the word "calm," without having to
go through the emptying technique every time.

DRIVING RANGE PRACTICE

нow many times have you seen someone at a
practice range hit nothing but woods? Very frequently,
I bet—despite the fact that this is truly one of the worst
things any golfer can do if he really wants to improve
his game.

Why? Well, although it is true that the golf swing is
essentially the same for each club, that doesn't prevent
golfers from varying their swings as they react instinctively to the physical shape and length of the varying
clubs. For example, an inexpert golfer may have very
little tendency to scoop with his driver, its flat face inviting anything but a scooping action. But, when he
looks down at the face of an 8 or 9 iron, there is a
strong likelihood that his instinctive response will be
to scoop at the ball to get it airborne, because of the
lofted club's scoop-like appearance.

One obvious way to overcome this tendency to unconsciously react to the club face is to use as many
clubs as possible in practice. Indeed, this is the only
way I know to develop and groove a basically sound
swing pattern that will work with every club.

There is another reason why golfers should never
hit continually with the same club or group of clubs.
In baseball the batter has three strikes before he's out,
but the golfer has only one swing at the ball at each
location, and almost always he must use a different
club each time. Thus, practicing continuously with
the same club is no way to prepare for the variety of
shots that one must face in actual play.

Another practice error of many golfers is hitting too
many balls at each session. They seem to feel that there

is some quantitative relationship between the number of balls they hit and the proficiency of their swings. But swinging the club the *wrong* way a hundred times only compounds the "wrongness." Again, it's that quest for magic—the hope that out of the ashes of endless practice shots will emerge the phoenix of a golf swing that always propels the ball far and straight. Unfortunately, this metamorphosis never occurs.

If a golfer *really* means business, I think he should hit only a small bucket of balls at each practice session. Hitting one or two large buckets only exhausts most golfers, which sooner or later makes them sloppy physically and mentally. With only a small bucket of balls, the golfer senses that each one counts. He takes his time with each shot, getting the most out of it because the ball supply is limited. This may sound like reverse psychology, but it isn't. The golfer has to include some element in his practice that will instill in his mind the fact that each shot in golf has a unique importance of its own, and frugality is one way to do this.

One of the symptoms of "golf rangitis" is that the golfer hits furiously, but not to any specific target. Oh, sure, there may be a bull's-eye out there at 200 yards, but he doesn't really shoot "at" it. What he tries to do is shoot *past* it, because that makes the hairs grow on his chest. But *ball control*, which is the ultimate theme of the game, is directly related to *club-head control*, which is best achieved with a specific target image in mind. Obviously, therefore, every time you strike the ball, it should be with some specific target in mind. By leaving this element out of your practice sessions you may be getting exercise, but you surely are not improving your golf.

LEARNING THE "SLING" FEELING

ONE factor that makes it difficult for the golfer to accept the idea of the golf swing as a "sling" is that most slings are made of leather, rubber, or some other pliable material. The sling in golf consists of the arms and the extension of the arms, namely the club shaft, but it is difficult for the golfer to accept the stiff metal club shaft as a rope or a sling. In fact, much is written about the effect of different kinds of shafts, the idea being that the stiffness of the shaft may in some way hold the secret to distance.

The truth, however, is that for the golfer to generate maximum centrifugal force in his golf swing, he must think of the club shaft as something soft and malleable, like a rope. Indeed, one of the best ways to establish the feel of a good golf swing is to swing a small weight, tied to the end of a rope, in the same way that you would swing a golf club.

Immediately you will discover how necessary it is for your muscles to *wait* for that weight to swing back; and how your shoulders must turn in a way that gives time for that mass to get up to an optimal position for slinging; and how your legs must lead the downswing while your arms *wait* for the mass to accelerate; and how all of your movements focus on that point on the ground that you are attempting to swing *through;* and how beautifully your head stays steady; and how aware of the path of the club head your mind remains long after it has swung through the target area.

It really isn't necessary to rig up this kind of apparatus to experience these feelings. You have an imagination—use it. Simply imagine that the club shaft is a rope and that the club head is a weight hanging at the end of it. You're now going to sling that weight in such a way that it travels at maximum velocity at a selected angle of decline, along a path that leads momentarily straight to a distant target, with a part of that weight facing that target.

If you can translate that imagery into movement, I promise your golf will improve immediately beyond your wildest dreams. It isn't something that can be done overnight, but once it's grooved it will never go away again. Until you have reached that state, however, you will not play the game up to your full potential. Until you totally familiarize yourself with these feelings, you will always be preoccupied with the uncertainty of a swing that can go haywire under the least kind of stress.

THE USE OF IMAGERY

THERE are other ways you can apply your imagination to help yourself. You may be standing in your backyard swinging at a plastic ball full of holes, but that doesn't mean that that is where your mind has to be. You can visualize any hole on any course you desire, and it won't cost a nickel.

For example, you may actually be standing in your backyard looking at your neighbor's garbage pails, but in your own mind you are on a high promontory in the Alps, standing on the tee, with a slight wind from the right. Far below, looking like a postage stamp, is the green. If you play the shot just right, with a nice easy swing, you can reach that distant target, even though the card reads 300 yards. You know the temptation is to try to hit too hard. You remind yourself that the velocity of the club head is related not to how "hard" you swing the club, but rather to the *efficiency* with which you swing it. You know how heavily your level of efficiency rests on getting all of that tension out of your muscles, and you take time to do this. Then you make your move: smooth, coordinated, with no sense of rushing. The club head builds up momentum in its own time and comes through the ball square, at the precise angle of approach, in line with the target, at top velocity. The ball sails off into the clear mountain air. You've played it slightly to the right. The breeze brings the ball back on line with the target. It's a beautiful shot. It hits the lid of the middle garbage can dead center, or that beautiful postage-stamp green in Switzerland—whichever you prefer.

Some people may think that using the imagination in this way is a little silly, but if they ever experienced its benefits such reservations would quickly disappear. This kind of practice experience in your imagination teaches you to confront and overcome the psychic hazards that precipitate fear and uncertainty. If you can make yourself practice in this way two or three times a week, you will soon find that you can approach *any* golfing situation with a totally different attitude. When you look out at that scene that previously filled you with anxiety, you will feel a warm sense of familiarity. You will know exactly how to swing the club because you've done it dozens of times in your own backyard.

This is the best way I know both of developing the "feel" of the correct golf swing and of overcoming fear of playing any particular shot. If you can't manage it, then you could always try psychoanalysis, but at $75 a session, five times a week, it can be a pretty costly learning experience. And there's always the chance that you might end up learning that your golfing anxieties are based upon an illicit desire to do away with your old man!

FACING THE REALITIES

AT any practice range, whether it be the kind that uses rubber mats for tees and slabs of plastic for grass, or a country club range with all the simulated conditions of a golf course, the golfer always plays from a preferred lie.

Now, we all know that the only preferred lie on the golf course itself is on the tee—in *real* golf you have to play the ball as it lies, unless there is some valid extenuating circumstance. The only way out of that fear-provoking situation is "winter rules," and it is simply because they alleviate fear that these rules have become so popular. Indeed, many golfers are now so saturated with this dogma that they are compelled to alter every lie they encounter, even the good ones, on the basis that any lie is unpreferable until they have changed it.

Unfortunately, this approach is one of the main reasons so many people are comparatively successful on the range, but dismal failures at scoring on the course. They have practiced, certainly, but not in a way that prepares them to deal with the realities of the game.

It is therefore essential that the golfer who really wants to improve confront in practice as many unpreferred lies as possible. He should not always hit the ball from a perfectly horizontal lie. He should practice from areas where the ground slants up or down, or from side to side. If he can't find sloping ground on the golf range, then he should get out to a city park or a corner lot (if there are any left!) and practice there.

In the same way, it isn't going to do him any harm to practice from those other realities of real golf, rough and sand. And he might also confront the weather: a little wind offers beautiful practice conditions, as does occasional drizzle or light rain. If you play golf seriously there are going to be many occasions on which you're going to have to deal with both. The fact that most golfers don't have that capability is an indication of their general insecurity about their golfing prowess —and often a reflection of insecurity in other areas of their lives.

PUTTING

THE least-practiced part of golf is putting. There is really no excuse for this, but there are some pretty obvious reasons behind it. To most golfers, putting is self-indulgent—something people do on cruises, or little old ladies dabble at on the finely manicured greens of fashionable resort hotels. There is, therefore, an ingrained sense of contempt for a part of the game that is generally considered less than manly. This, of course, is delusional thinking, for as we've noted before, putting has broken more brave men than any other part of the game.

The putting stroke as a gymnastic maneuver is no-where nearly so complicated as the full swing. The stroke is short and contained, and the club head never leaves the field of vision, which makes its path far easier to control than on full shots. Thus, the most important ingredient in putting is not mechanics but "feel"—the *feel* of the *movement* of the club head *through* the ball.

There is no magic way to get that feel. The only way to achieve it is by putting as many balls as you can from a variety of distances, on greens that slope, or where the grain goes in different directions.

When you are in the process of acquiring overall feel for distance on a green, you should putt several balls from the same spot. But, once you have that feel, you should practice with only one ball at a time, because all your practice should remind you of the fact that you have only one crack at the ball in "real" golf.

Also, don't forget the short putts. More golfers have been destroyed by short putts than long ones, yet most people I see practicing putting seem to be interested only in the fifteen-footers or longer. If they miss the cup by six feet, they hurry on to the next putt. If they miss by three feet, they don't even bother to hole out.

Putts on the course are usually made—or missed— under pressure. Is there any way that this factor can be introduced into putting practice? The answer is that it can be done once again through the medium of your imagination. When you putt on the course in a *game* of golf you've usually got two, three, or more strokes behind you on the hole. If you are playing a par-4 hole and are on in three, there is a lot of pressure on you to sink the putt for par. If you are on in two, there may be even more pressure to sink the putt for a birdie. If you are on in four, there is pressure to get down in one putt and save both your overall score and your self-respect. So putting in the game is essentially a sequel or aftermath experience.

Now, when you are on the practice putting green, or even on the living-room rug putting to the mouth of a tumbler or a chair leg, there is nothing functional that has gone on beforehand. The putt in a sense is an isolated incident and an end unto itself. This is what needs to be overcome, and the way to do it is to set up an imaginary situation.

Imagine, for example, that you have reached the green in four on a par-4 hole. You lost one shot in the woods and your third shot caught the bunker. You've now got to sink this putt to save bogey. There is plenty of stress in a real-life situation of this kind, and a lot of it can be captured through your imagination. As you focus your imagination on this situation, you will begin to feel the anxiety mounting, a sense of tension in your muscles. These are great elements to deal with in practice, because they wreak so much havoc in "real" golf. Here is an opportunity to confront that old bogy, anxiety, and the more successful you become in coping with it in practice, the easier it becomes for you to deal with it on the course.

Your mind—more specifically your *imagination*—can be extremely helpful to you in acquiring the muscular and mental skills that make for good golf. Most golfers waste their time in practice, often only compounding the errors that are already plaguing them. If they would only use a fraction of their imagination, they could gain not only mechanical skills, but also learn to deal with the psychological traumas that will destroy every golfer if left unchecked.

10

The Special Problems
of Women Golfers

THE AURA OF MASCULINE HOSTILITY

GOLF has been essentially a man's game. It wasn't until well into this century that many women dared venture onto the golf course. We don't know who the first American woman golfer was, but one thing is for sure—she was certainly brave. Since the beginning of the game the specter of masculinity has hung over most golf courses like a heavy fog, and dealing with this masculine atmosphere is one of the female golfer's major mental chores.

The aura of masculinity pervades the history of golf and colors every aspect of the game. The people who write about golf are mostly men, and, of course, they write from the perspective they know best, which is the masculine one. Nearly all golf teachers are men, and although I do know male instructors who handle women pupils very well, there are some who use a note of condescension in their instruction to women—

their male prejudice is too much for them to contain.

Some women, detecting this hostility, will retaliate with a display of incompetence that is not totally sincere. The more hopeless they become in their responses, the more futile become the male's attempts at instruction. Many times, below the level of consciousness, a very subtle but fierce warfare rages between a woman and a male instructor.

On the course, women are subject to much less subtle blasts of male hostility. Men are often infuriated when they find themselves behind a female foursome, no matter how competent the players may be. Nothing much is ever said, but the waves of repressed hostility rise ever higher the closer the male group gets to the female group. Very often the women, alive to this hostile atmosphere, eventually let the "big hitters" through. It's all done with an air of politeness, but if you can be objective, you just *know* that the men don't think the women should be there at all.

If that situation is the most infuriating to both sexes, the one that is the most threatening to the male is the sight of a fast-playing female twosome roaring up from behind. If you ever want to catalyze the reactions of a slow-moving male foursome, just slip a pair of fast-playing females in behind them. The males will start playing so fast that you can't even keep up with them in a golf cart. Many male golfers will do almost anything to avoid being passed by women golfers.

It is my belief that a woman should not try to deny the presence of either subtle or overt male disapproval on the golf course. She must simply accept it as part of the reality that she has to deal with if she's going to play golf. She should not allow the aura of masculinity to turn her from the game. But she must realize that it's there and be on the lookout for any negative re-actions on her own part in response to it. She can take strength from the fact that, in the past few years, women have come into their own in golf, and that this trend will continue, irrespective of anything that men may consciously or unconsciously wish they could do to prevent it.

POWER VERSUS PRECISION

WOMEN are not as physically strong as men. I doubt if there will ever be a female all-American full-back, or a serious female contender for the heavyweight boxing crown and, what's more, it's my belief that few women ever entertain such ambitions.

From the cradle on, man's fantasy life is constantly fed with dreams of power: George and the Dragon, Jack the Giant Killer, Robin Hood, the Knights of the Round Table, and so on. Dreams of power and aggression are an important part of the development of the male mind, so it is understandable that power should creep into all the male-invented games. In actuality, the tendency to stand in awe of power prevents many a man from ever trying his best to master a game like golf: it's a very humiliating experience for a man to follow onto the tee someone who has just hit a ball 250 yards, knowing he can't hit it more than 175.

Women don't cherish this power myth, and as a result can play a game like golf within their limitations much better than men. One sees women golfers who can hit a ball a long way, but almost without exception they do it with graceful finesse. And that's a valid approach. When Nicklaus really gets into a ball, the power surge makes you shudder—there is something in that crunch that makes you break out in goose bumps. We may all be impressed by this flamboyant show of strength, but a woman may not be able to match it, and there is no reason why she should feel inferior because she doesn't have such massive power at her disposal.

If a woman golfer worries less about power, she will be freer to apply herself to the precision aspects of the game. She can strive primarily to hit the ball accurately, with distance her second goal, whereas most men *always* strive primarily for distance, with accuracy very much a secondary concern. Finesse—meaning precision, timing, tempo—is her key to success. In the final analysis what matters in golf is the number of strokes you take, not how far you hit the ball.

Women can become just as good golfers as men if they work with what they've got. It's when they try to become "men golfers" that they get in trouble, and the idea that one has to project a very masculine image is off-putting to many would-be women golfers. Marlene Hagge and Laura Baugh are totally feminine golfers. They play entirely within their capabilities and bring a grace and beauty to golf that is a pleasure to behold.

Many women hesitate to use the wood clubs because they seem more ponderous than the irons and appear to demand the reserves of strength that men have more readily at their disposal. It's not what the clubs *look like* that's important, however, it's the *way they are used*. Woods really aren't that bulky, and fitted into a woman's particular style and tempo, woods will work just as well for her as any other club in the bag.

INVOLVEMENT

WOMEN generally don't become as seriously involved with golf as do many men. Men often actually fall "in love" with golf; become infatuated with it; let it take precedence over everything else in their lives; eat, sleep, and drink it. As a result, they spend more time at golf than women, and therefore become better players. I have only very rarely seen women become totally infatuated with golf; yet they usually have more free time to play and practice—they should take full advantage of it if they really seek improvement. The better they are at golf, the more involved they will become, and the more involved they become, the better they will be.

EXCESSIVE CAUTION AND DEPENDENCE

WOMEN generally play golf with much more caution than men. The male golfer will take a chance. The female golfer will more often take the safe way. By making themselves take a few more chances, women generally score better.

On the other hand, the woman's caution generally makes her more consistent in her scoring. Many males vary fifteen to twenty strokes from game to game, but women rarely vary more than five to ten strokes. Yet the hard fact remains that the woman who wants to score lower has got to make herself take more chances.

Women also depend too much on their caddies. To most men, caddies get paid to carry the bag. Women golfers, however, sometimes tend to look upon their caddies as mentors. I've seen women, playing their home courses, who always ask the caddie if they have made the right club selection, or who will even demand that he make the selection for them. The caddies often become carried away with this attention and begin offering advice even when it isn't asked for, which has thrown more than one woman golfer off her game.

We have said previously that golf is a very lonely game. Perhaps it's that characteristic that compels some women to involve their caddies. However, the sooner a player faces the fact that golf *is* a lonely game, and thereby learns to make his or her own decisions about it, the better this player is going to perform.

There is certainly nothing wrong with asking your caddie his opinion about a situation if you feel he may have enough practical knowledge of the course to offer some useful information. But *you* should then make the ultimate decision. The more you make your own decisions, the more confident you become about your ability to handle every situation on the course. Confidence is one of the greatest attributes any golfer can have. It can't be bought, but it can be earned, and you earn it by making and then implementing your own decisions.

HAZARDS

WOMEN generally overreact to hazards. The threat of a hazard often compels a woman to try a circuitous route to the green, even at the cost of a couple of extra strokes on the way.

Despite this tendency to recoil from hazards, the woman with reasonable physical agility can learn to come out of sand or light rough as effectively as most men, because these are situations requiring finesse rather than power. All most women need to do to become proficient in getting out of sand is to strive to make the club flow gracefully through it and under the ball.

THE SWING

THE golf swing, as we have previously mentioned, is learned primarily by imitation. For a woman, nine times out of ten, this means imitating the moves of a male instructor.

Now, it is very difficult for any instructor, no matter how sympathetic to women, to present a totally valid physical example for a woman to emulate. In the first place, he is a lot stronger than she is, which makes the action physically easier for him. In the second place, he doesn't have her physical equipment in the pectoral areas, so how can he really understand about compensating for something that he doesn't possess? This discrepancy is obviously accentuated in the case of the big-bosomed woman, who really can't swing the club like a man or a smaller woman.

A woman is usually aware of these discrepancies. But if she wants to improve, she tries very hard to imitate the instructor. The result, very often, is that she tries *too* hard. Her muscles stiffen with stress and uncertainty; she swings the club determinedly, but with a grim sense of futility. Indeed, many women, trying too hard to reach the unreachable goal of making their swings just like a man's, become stiff and jerky in their moves.

The only sure way for a woman to overcome this is to understand that power in the golf swing does not come from muscular contraction, but rather from balance and leverage. The ideal swing model for a woman, therefore, is not Arnold Palmer driving into a headwind, but the smooth and graceful motions of the women professionals.

Women have a great advantage in that, generally speaking, they do not need to deal with so many strong images from past athletic experiences that can destroy the purity of their swings. The hitting games—baseball, handball, hockey—that many men play establish patterns that greatly inhibit the type of motion necessary for good golf. In fact, 90 percent of the men who fail at golf do so because, halfway through the action, they unconsciously abandon the image of the true golf swing for a more forceful type of hitting motion with which they've become familiar in earlier days. This type of regression is rare among women, simply because fewer women have hit baseballs, chopped wood or swung axes. As a result, women generally do not have to deal with the established patterns of muscle usage developed by most males. Their approach can be purer, which offers them the chance to learn the correct swing far more easily than can the average man.

It is especially difficult to teach middle-aged men the golf swing. They are not old enough to be humble and submissive, nor are they young enough to be eager and suggestible. They are set in their ways. They think they know as much as the professional but are angry because they can't implement the swing in the same way. This is why most older male golfers don't often go to a pro, and don't stick with him very long if they do. They fashion the swing to their own ideas. They consider all this stuff about swing dynamics a lot of nonsense. They are too tightly bound up with memories of athletic experience to which the golf swing seems contradictory.

Older women rarely have this problem. They may share all the problems of women golfers in general, but as golf students they are usually not impeded by previous athletic experiences. The older woman also generally pays more attention to her pro's advice, which makes her a more receptive student than the middle-aged man, who often harbors the secret thought that he could have outkicked this guy by at least thirty yards if they were playing football twenty-five years ago.

SELF-CONSCIOUSNESS

WOMEN are often more self-conscious than men on the golf course. They are especially terrified on the tee, where they feel in the center of the stage with the spotlight fully on them. They are also often terrified by caddies, who they feel know all the mysterious secrets of this game and are secretly contemptuous of their efforts. Stage fright sometimes becomes so intense that all they want to do is get out of that spotlight as quickly as possible. The result is a quick swipe at the ball in the hope of some kind of contact that will let them escape that cruel stage.

In such situations, women golfers clearly are caught

up in the Ego defense of "projection"—that is, they are projecting their insecurities onto others. In most situations, there is no way a person can be certain of what another is thinking unless it's expressed verbally. A woman may think her caddie is smirking at her because of her unorthodox swing, whereas actually he may be thinking about a joke one of the boys told him last night.

The way to overcome this problem of self-consciousness is first to realize that it exists, which takes the whole process out of the realm of the mysterious. Your main concern on the tee can then become: "What am I going to do with the ball?" And, in that respect, the more you understand the golf swing and each of its component parts, the less opportunity your mind will have to become involved with egocentric thoughts that produce the painful self-consciousness that destroys any chance of a good swing.

BALL-ORIENTEDNESS

WOMEN golfers seem to be more ball-oriented than goal-oriented. Here again we are talking about a mental problem that afflicts all golfers, and that to my mind is a symptom of the tremendous emphasis that golf teachers have placed on the swing itself as an exercise in aesthetics.

The danger here is of "not seeing the forest for the trees," of becoming so engrossed with the swing *as a* swing that one forgets one is playing a game that depends on how few strokes are made, not on how beautiful one's swing looks. There are lots of golfers who score well with bad-looking swings, and some with great swings who can't break 90. This doesn't mean that you shouldn't try to perfect your swing. You should, but *without* getting so hung up on that objective that you forget the real object of the swing, which is to reach a specific target in a minimum number of shots.

One reason men are generally more goal-oriented in golf than women may be that they usually play for money, whereas women rarely seem to bet on their play. Betting, even though the sum may be nominal, is a definite spur to scoring well, in that to most people acquiring money is good and losing it bad. Many men thus play "better than their swings," especially when they are betting on themselves. I'm not advocating here that women become gamblers, but simply that they be more competitive: they should never cease to remind themselves that they are playing a game in which the primary purpose is to get the ball into the hole with the fewest number of strokes, not simply to swing the club attractively.

Golf is *not* intrinsically a man's game: a woman has as much claim to it as a man. But women should play like women; by utilizing the restraint, control, precision, and gracefulness that are their strongest points in the game. Let these attributes enhance their game, and they won't have to make excuses to anybody.

I I

The Right (and Wrong) Way to Talk to Yourself

Most people think of golf as a "quiet" game. The audience is generally under control, giving expression to circumspect demonstrations of enthusiasm only when golfers make exceptional shots. And when the golfer is in the process of making a swing, nobody in the audience would dare utter a word, or even clear his throat. Golfers talk to one another, but rarely with enthusiasm, because most of their dialogue is going on inside. In fact, they talk more to themselves than to anyone else on the course.

Many people will smile at that statement, because they imagine that people who talk to themselves end up in strait jackets in back wards of state hospitals. This, of course, is rarely true. If it were, there would be more people inside hospitals than outside. The fact is that we *all* talk more to ourselves than we do to other people, and it is only when we do this out loud that people raise their eyebrows. But to see people muttering to themselves on the golf course is not uncommon. In fact, it occurs so often that most of us just take it for granted.

THE INTERNAL DIALOGUE

MOST of the internal dialogue on the golf course is determined by the fate of the golf ball. If the ball remains on the fairway or green, the internal conversation is usually minimal; the golfer is either saying nice things to himself or saying nothing at all. However, when the ball finds its way into one of the forbidden areas, such as the rough or the sand, the internal dialogue flares up like a freshly stoked fire. Indeed, one often gets the feeling that if there was a device that could record these internal conversations, they would make the Watergate tapes sound like a Sunday-school lesson.

There is something implicit in the game of golf that can make men and women extremely angry. Primarily it's because in golf there is no way we can throw up smoke screens to cover our inner deficiencies. I don't believe there is another sport in which the participant is so completely exposed. Nor is there a sport in which the player's skill can vary so much from day to day, or, for that matter, from moment to moment. Golf is a game of man against himself, and that may be the reason for the intensity of the anger it creates. In golf, man can't justify directing that anger at anyone but himself.

The intense emotional responses provoked by the game are, then, self-directed, and very often in language that would wither the ears of a deck hand. It seems that in golf man is ever ready to condemn himself. The golfer would never talk to another person as harshly as he talks to himself, or criticize another person as subjectively and unfairly as he criticizes himself. Sometimes there seems to be no form of speech adequate to express the fierceness of his hostility toward himself. Very often a man who is perfectly contained in other areas of life regresses to such a level that only nonverbal groanings find their way to his vocal chords.

PERFECTIONISM VERSUS TRYING FOR PERFECTION

ALL athletes can become angry with themselves, largely because their demands for perfection are so stringent. The flaw in their thinking is their lack of understanding of the difference between perfectionism and *trying* for perfection. The perfectionist's problem is not that he strives for perfection, but rather that he *expects* perfection. When he doesn't get it, he explodes with anger. Also, his perfectionism is linked with his sense of self-worth. His criterion for self-acceptance is good performance, and if he fails to achieve it he rejects himself.

The early life histories of most perfectionists show that a pattern of perfectionism began because they were insecure about the amount of love they were getting from their parents. Unconsciously, they began to rely upon performance to gain that acceptance. What they did not understand is that acceptance for what they "can do" is not the same as acceptance for "what they are." This type of person is, then, "afraid" to be what he is, because it may not be good enough. This fear can establish an undercurrent of dislike or resentment of others. Ultimately, when such a person applies this attitude to his dealings with himself, the self-resentment intensifies his feelings of anger and precipitates a blistering internal dialogue.

There are no magic formulas for getting rid of something as deep-seated as perfectionism. The golfer, however, must first recognize it as an undesirable aspect of his personality that is interfering with his ability to enjoy the game. Above all, however, he must realize that the failing lies not in the *pursuit* of perfection, but only in *expecting* its achievement.

Primarily, the golfer must accept that he is human, and that one of the characteristics of the human state is making mistakes. Sinless perfection is no more attainable on the golf course than in man's spiritual life. The golfer must have available in his verbal equipment thoughts and words that can counter his surges of perfectionism. He must learn to talk to himself as he would to his best friend, because in a very real sense he is his own best friend. If a close friend was trying very hard to achieve a difficult task, you wouldn't browbeat him if he failed. You'd be kind, sympathetic, and understanding, you would encourage and console him. Yet how many golfers call themselves "stupid idiots," and worse, and *mean* it, whenever they hit anything less than a 100 percent perfect shot. The basic problem such people face is that, in their desire for achievement, they forget that they are human.

BELIEVING IN YOURSELF

ONE of the marks of a great achiever is never giving up. No matter how discouraging his situation, he never stops believing in himself. He must, therefore, be telling himself some very encouraging things. He can rarely be maligning himself in his inner dialogue. Instead, he devotes his energy to determining the reason for his shortcoming, *without* casting any aspersions on his own character.

To the great golfer, the *game* is the most important thing. His own worth as a result of the game is secondary. One proof of this is the great player's respect for the game. He has as much respect for a 6-inch putt as for a 300-yard drive, and he knows that he will always make mistakes on both. That's a form of humility most average golfers don't have—and need.

STAYING IN STEP WITH TIME

MOST golfers allow their emotions to vacillate violently. After a great shot, there is a tendency to become elated, which often breeds carelessness on the next shot. After a poor shot depression sets in, which breeds lack of effort on the next shot.

The golfer must be aware of these fluctuations and be ready to deal with them by continually reminding himself that the most important shot is the one he is about to make, and also that this is the only time in his life he will be able to make *that* particular shot under *these* specific conditions. The concept of living one day at a time—the basic philosophy of Alcoholics Anonymous—is accentuated on the golf course, where the golfer must live each moment at a time. *Now* is the only time that matters.

Time is always a difficult problem for human beings to deal with. Often we wish that we could skip over it, especially if the going is rough, but we know from bitter experience that this is impossible. We have to be in step with time. Every golfer has wished at the end of seven or eight holes of good golf that he could leap over all of the rest of the holes, especially a particular hole that always gives him trouble. But it cannot happen. He has to plug away at each hole as it comes along, continually striving to keep himself in the present. There is just no "other time" that you can play this game, or live this life.

In this respect, the golfer must try to talk himself into his own ideal physical and emotional tempo. He must not be too hurried, nor too deliberately slow, and he must recognize the "feel" of his own most comfortable tempo, so that when he deviates from it he can recognize the deviation and talk himself gently back into step again.

FINDING GOOD THINGS TO SAY ABOUT YOURSELF

THE golfer must always find good things to say to himself on the golf course. The flow of positive thinking must never cease.

Take a golfer whose ball just catches the lip of a trap and falls back into the sand instead of rolling onto the green. For many, the first response to this experience is, "You stupid moron, why didn't you hit it just a little bit harder?" The *fact* of the matter is that he did not hit it a little bit harder. And there is no way to go back and do it over again. The ball rests in the sand and there is only one person who's going to be able to do anything about that. What might have happened is totally irrelevant. The golfer now has a new problem, a new challenge. And obviously this "now" challenge demands and deserves as much time as, and even more consideration than, if the ball were sitting up on a tuft of grass in the middle of the fairway.

When you don't fight the rush of negative thinking that comes into your mind when something like this happens to your ball, by talking encouragingly to yourself, you're compounding your error. Some of the most magnificent shots that you will see in tournaments are from undesirable lies. This is because the champion golfer meets the challenge of adversity. He is able to close all the doubts and fears out of his mind, and to mobilize all of his skill and knowledge to produce an effective shot after having played a less than effective shot.

As opposed to this professional approach, how many times have you seen average golfers rush into the sand, or some other undesirable spot on the golf course, as though they were going to put out a fire. The only thought in their minds is, "Let's get this over with as quickly as possible." They lash savagely at the ball, trying to punish it, hoping that the sheer power of their blows will lift it to the green from which it had no right to wander in the first place.

All of the primitive instincts that have been hibernating in a man's "civilized" mind come rushing to the forefront of his awareness in this kind of situation. The only words the golfer can tolerate are: "Hurry!" "Explode!" "Get it out at all costs!" Fear creeps into the picture, amplifying the inner chaos. The thought "What if it doesn't get out?" reinforces the urge to hit even harder. In his turmoil of mind the golfer can hardly distinguish between sand and ball, and as a result he scoops a great deal of sand and very little ball. The ball, like as not, remains in the sand, and the golfer wishes with all his might that these next excruciating moments could be eliminated from his life. But he knows he's got to "bite the bullet." He glances around at the other members of the foursome for some form of compassion. They all seem to be looking in different directions, occupied with something else. Sensing the embarrassment they are fighting, he finds no comfort there.

THE HUMAN RIGHT TO MAKE MISTAKES

WE'VE all seen golfers caught up in this convulsion of frustration. None of its agony would have been necessary if the golfer had taken charge of his internal dialogue. The golfer who talks to himself in the "right" way operates from the basic premise that, above all else, he is human, which gives him the right to make mistakes. And that's what a golfer really must do—deal with his own "humanness." He must accept the bad lies, the sand, the rough as part of the challenge of the game, *trying* for perfection, but never *expecting* it. Only then can he respond positively to overcoming his own inevitable mistakes.

To do this, the golfer must be very kind and understanding to himself. Like a mentor to his favorite pupil, he must talk to himself encouragingly: "You can do it. Just take it easy. Give your body time to do what it's capable of doing. Nobody's rushing you. You can do it." He must learn to take charge of his internal dialogue, learn to tune out the static, learn not to be defeated by himself, learn to get his mind working *for* himself, not *against* himself. Golf is more than whacking a ball around the course. It's dealing with a unique human situation—man pitted against himself.

Your ultimate fate on the golf course depends to a great extent upon the character of your internal dialogue. So learn to treat yourself like a friend. Learn some words of self-encouragement, talk to yourself gently and with kindness. Out of this will come a belief that you can handle any golfing situation. It's a dialogue that must be rooted in *reality*, not in dreams. You may end up finding you are your own best friend. And when that happens, your golf can't do anything else but get better.

12

Nine Holes with a Shrink on Your Shoulder

THE idea of playing nine holes of golf with a "shrink" on their shoulder would be enough to put a lot of golfers in a stait jacket. However, there are many who might learn something by watching a psychiatrist bird-dog some poor victim around the course.

The victim we've chosen for this exercise is a "fluctuating" 18 handicapper. Some days he shoots in the low eighties. Other days he's lucky to break 100. He suffers at golf not because he lacks physical ability, but because he does not realize that the golfer needs to deal with feelings and negative attitudes just as much as with bad lies and hazards. Perhaps if you follow this fellow around nine holes you will begin to appreciate the dimensions of the golfer's prcblems and, hopefully, discover some better ways of dealing with them. In the dialogue portions that follow, the letter "G" indicates the golfer, "S" the shrink.

HOLE NUMBER 1

Golfer and shrink walk to the first hole, an easy par-4, 340 yards long. The tee is elevated about fifty feet above the fairway. If the golfer gets a good drive in the fairway the ball will roll a long way. If, however, he pushes his drive, it can finish in a deep pit to the right side of the fairway. If he pulls left, he can put the ball behind a couple of trees on that side of the fairway.

G: I hate hitting first. I feel so self-conscious.

S: You've got to hit it sometime, so what's the difference? What are you afraid of?

G: I'm not afraid of anything. I just don't want to make a fool of myself.

S: Why do you think you're going to make a fool of yourself? Your negative attitude almost condemns you to failure. Minds are very suggestible. *Thinking* success doesn't always produce success, but you'll seldom succeed if you *don't* think success. One of your major mental jobs as a golfer is to deal with that tremendous flood of negative thoughts that can break into your mind at any time. These negative thoughts work like the domino theory. If you let yourself become intimidated by hitting first, you'll unleash a whole series of negative thoughts. You'll allow resentment to creep into your swing. You'll abandon your tempo and lash out at the ball as though it were an embodiment of cruel fate. So be on the lookout for any negative attitude and replace it with a positive thought. Imagine making a good drive. That positive image will then fill your mind and leave no room for any other negative thoughts.

G: I still feel nervous. I can't get rid of that tense feeling. My muscles feel stiff. The club feels strange in my hands.

S: Tension is something you can do something about once you recognize it. Those stiff, nervous feelings are an indication that your body's beginning to fill up with anxiety. If you don't learn to do something about it, that 18 handicap of yours is going to skyrocket to 38.

G: What can I do about it? You haven't got an extra tranquilizer on you, have you, Doc?

S: That's the trouble with so many people in the world today. They want a pill to do something that their bodies can do a lot better. You've got an imagination—*use* it. Think of your body as a vessel filled with liquid tension. Now let that fluid drain downward, from the top of your head, through your forehead, neck, and shoulders. Move those shoulders around to confirm the fact that they're becoming nice and loose. Now let the fluid drain out of your arms, right down through your hands and fingers. Next let that tension drain out of your chest and slowly down through your abdomen. Feel it go down through your hips and legs. Kick your feet as if you were shaking it out of your toes. Move your body around to prove to yourself how supple it now is. Take a couple of easy swings with the club. How does that feel?

G: Feels great, but how long will it last?

S: That's up to you. One of your main jobs in this game is to be on the lookout for excessive tension just as much as you are for water hazards. Now, go ahead and make your shot.

G: I hate this driver.

S: How come you use it, then?

G: I know if I could learn to hit it right I could get an extra twenty-five yards.

S: What are your odds of hitting it well on this shot?

G: Pretty long, but I know I could hit it straight with my 3 wood.

S: Then use your 3 wood. The idea of this game is to use the best equipment that you've got to get the ball into the hole in the least number of strokes. That's why you're allowed fourteen clubs. Don't practice during a game. Learning and playing are not compatible activities. Keep the driver in your bag until you've practiced with it enough to use it with confidence. In this game you've got to begin with knowns and work toward unknowns. If you begin with unknowns you're going to go nowhere real fast.

The golfer takes a few quick swings to get the feel of his 3-wood club and then steps up to the ball. His practice swing looked smooth and rhythmical, but his actual swing is much faster. The ball flies off to the right and lands in the grass-lined cavity about 175 yards away.

S: How do you feel?

G: Rotten.

S: Do you feel angry?

G: I sure do. How could anybody be so stupid?

S: What did you do that was stupid?

G: I hit it into that ridiculous pit.

S: Why is that stupid?

G: I knew the pit was there and I hit it into it anyway. Doesn't that strike you as being stupid?

S: No. Just because you made a bad swing doesn't mean you're mentally deficient.

G: Yeah, but you should have seen the way I was hitting my 3 woods just before the game—fifteen in a row, each 230 straight as an arrow. It doesn't make any sense!

S: How you practice doesn't really have much bearing on how you'll play. Don't kid yourself into believing that you *deserve* to play well because you practiced well. Practice makes you ball-oriented rather than target-oriented. I've known people who've practiced three times a week for years and have still never broken 90. One reason is that they are totally ball-oriented. They bring the practice range with them onto the golf course, but that doesn't work, because on the golf range if you make a bad shot you've always got another ball waiting for you in the pail. In the game of golf you only get one shot in each situation.

Golfer and shrink descend into the pit. The ball is on a nice uphill lie. But at the top of the pit is a small tree that blocks direct access to the green. The golfer can play out to the right, where he has to clear a bunker, or left, which lands him in front of the green for an easy chip shot.

S: What are you going to do?

G: If I were Nicklaus I'd go over the tree with an 8 iron.

S: Well, you're not Nicklaus, so we can forget about that. An 18 handicapper hasn't got that kind of talent. If he did he wouldn't be an 18 handicapper. Golf is a game of odds, and the more realistic you are about your talent, the better you'll be at making those odds work in your favor.

The golfer finally elects to play left of the tree. He strikes his 5-iron solidly and his ball finishes just short of the green, from where he chips close to the hole and sinks his putt for a par.

HOLE NUMBER 2

This hole is 200 yards, par-3. The green is well-guarded by bunkers, except directly in front. The big hitters use a long iron from the tee, but most golfers must use woods. The big hitter in our group has just dropped his 2-iron shot eight feet from the pin. Our golfer is looking through his bag for the right club. He selects the 3 wood.

S: What are you frowning for? Something seems to be bothering you.

G: Did you see that guy drop that one on with a 2 iron? I'll be lucky to get there with a 3 wood.

S: Don't let yourself get hung up on the other person's game. He's got his own problems, you've got yours. By comparing yourself negatively with him, you are, in effect, putting yourself down. This again is further evidence of the negative feedback I've been talking about. Play your game with what you've got. What's your strategy on this hole?

G: Well, the hole is a little over 200 yards. I know I can hit it that far if I get into it right.

S: That's what I call "driving range mentality."

G: What does that mean?

S: It means that if you're on the driving range, and you've got a target 200 yards away, you're going to "go" for it. If your first three balls go to the right, you make some adjustment in your swing and go at it with another ball. But there you don't have to follow up a bad shot with another from a bunker. Remember that now you're in a *game*. The club you choose on one shot affects your chances on the next. What are the odds of your dropping one on the green with that 3 wood?

G: I did it twice last year.

S: That makes the odds fairly long, doesn't it? You see, on this shot you obviously need accuracy as well as distance. If you're off line you know for sure you're going to be in a bunker, behind a tree, or in that unplayable rough on the left. So what's your safest wood—the one you feel you can hit the straightest?

G: I guess the 5 wood, but I could never get there with a 5 wood.

S: Who's talking about "getting there"? What's wrong with hitting one twenty yards short? That will put you in great shape for a clear pitch shot or even a chip, and you'll be sure to play it from fairway instead of sand.

G: You're going to have me playing old man's golf. I'm not ready for the rocking chair yet!

The golfer slices his 5 wood slightly, but the shot finishes safely short of the sand. He pitches to fifteen feet left of the flagstick and makes two putts for an easy four.

HOLE NUMBER 3

This hole is a long, 400-yard par-4. The tee is elevated, but the green is hidden. The first shot must be accurate to allow any chance for a clear second.

G: This hole always gives me the willies. If I come in with anything less than a double bogey, I consider it a good day.

S: What makes it so difficult?

G: Can't you see how many places you can go wrong from up here? If you top one you're in the gully. If you slice you're lost in the woods. And if you hook you might be stymied behind a tree.

S: You still haven't told me how many places you can go right.

G: What kind of double-talk is that? I've heard that you shrinks can make any simple problem complicated.

S: Listen, friend, I'm not involved in double-talk. I told you at the beginning of the game that one of your biggest mental hazards was negative thinking, and you've just swamped me with a flood of negative thoughts. You've told me all the ways you can go wrong on this hole. I want to know how many ways you can go right.

G: Well, the right way is obvious. It's a straight-ahead drive over that hump into the middle of the fairway. But that's some shot.

S: You mean you think it's a *long* shot?

G: I sure do. It's at least 200 yards and most of it carry.

S: How far do you think that hump is?

G: I don't know. Maybe 170 yards.

S: How high is the tee above the fairway?

G: Maybe seventy-five feet.

S: O.K. It doesn't seem to me that, with this much elevation, you need to worry about length. A seventy-five-foot elevation should give you an extra ten to twenty yards. The wily old Scotsman who laid out this course many years ago knew how men's hearts faint when they're exposed to this kind of a vista. He knew that the staggering height, the gaping gully, the thick forest on the right, and the line of poplars on the left can all create negative suggestions. What's happened to you is that the fear of the obstacles has led your mind into thinking a relatively easy shot is extremely difficult. You shouldn't have any trouble at all if you forget about the obstacles and think about driving the ball fairly straight.

The golfer gets off a nice drive. His second shot slides off to the right but finishes about fifteen yards from the green. The green rises rather sharply from front to back. The pin is about three-quarters of the way to the back of the green.

S: What are you going to use from there?

G: Guess I'll pitch it up with my trusty wedge. It's a little far for a run-up shot.

S: But the green slopes *upward*. If your pitch shot lands short, it will never run to the hole. A chip shot with a 6 iron would. And the chip is the safer shot because you don't need such a long swing. The shorter swing lessens your chances for error.

G: Well, thanks, Dr. Golf, but I still feel more confident with my wedge.

S: Then that's the club you should use, and don't let me or anybody else talk you out of it.

The golfer quickly steps up to the ball, swings the club back a trifle too far, and then sticks the blade into the ground behind the ball. The ball ineffectively slithers three feet off to the right. "Chilly-dipper!" shouts the big hitter from across the green. Our golfer develops a sick look.

S: You look pretty shaken up.

G: I'd like to kill that loud-mouth. He's so damn smug.

S: I warned you before not to get involved emotionally with the other players' games or comments. You're the one who pulled the boo-boo. What did you learn from it?

G: I guess I learned that I chilly-dipped. And I froze. I didn't let the tension out of my body.

S: You're right, but there are a couple of other things that happened as well. First, you played the shot far too quickly. Just because the ball is relatively close to the green doesn't mean that the shot is unimportant. One difference between a mediocre golfer and a good one is that the latter respects these short shots just as much as the long ones. Also, I'm quite *sure you didn't visualize* your shot beforehand. Where did you plan for the ball to land?

G: I didn't. I just tried to guess how hard to hit it.

S: You should always mentally visualize the proposed flight of the ball on every shot. This *has* to be part of your mental ritual. If you don't "see" a successful shot beforehand, you don't give your mind and body a positive goal.

The golfer takes care to visualize his next shot before he swings. His wedge catches the ball crisply. The shot lands a few feet short of the pin and rolls about a foot past for an easy tap-in bogey.

HOLE NUMBER 4

This is the first par-5 hole, 510 yards. The fairway is very wide, but the first impression is that the hole goes on forever. The flag is too distant to be seen from the tee. The problem here is chiefly dealing with distances that stretch out seemingly infinitely. The apprehension associated with dimensions like this makes the golfer's mind regress to a very primitive state. The doctor quickly senses the tension.

S: You seem preoccupied.

The golfer doesn't reply. He's too wrapped up in his mood.

S: I said, you seem preoccupied.

G: Yeah. This hole always spells disaster to me.

S: There you go with your negative thinking again. Remember, you've always got to be on the alert for it. Why do you think disaster on this hole?

G: My track record stinks. I made ten here once before. Maybe I can't get the ugly image out of my mind.

S: What did you learn from that humiliating experience?

G: I learned it's a tough hole. I went all to pieces. I came close to walking right off the course and never playing again.

S: If that's all you learned, you didn't learn much. What's the biggest problem on this hole?

G: That's kind of a ridiculous question. Distance, of course. This is where the big hitters really clean up. Musclebound over there will be home in two. I'll be lucky to get there in four.

S: Now I don't want you to get mad, but your statement sounds even more ridiculous than mine. How *long* is this hole?

G: Five hundred yards, more or less.

S: How much is 500 divided by four?

G: What is this? A golf game or a math class? It's 125 yards.

S: How much club do you need for 125 yards?

G: An 8 iron.

S: In other words, if you use the 8 iron four times in a row you could be on the green in four?

G: Yeah, that's *theoretically* correct.

S: So if you used your trusty 5 wood, which you can hit so accurately, you could be sitting about 140 yards from the green in two shots. A nice easy 6 or 7 iron would put you on the green in three.

G: That sounds great, but it doesn't always work that way.

S: How do you know? Have you ever tried?

G: Not really. What kind of a nut do you think I'd look like if I drove on a hole like this with a 5 wood? I'm telling you, these guys will be out there 225 yards and farther.

S: What's that got to do with *your* game? I'll say it again; you've *got* to play the game with what *you've* got and forget the other guy and his game. Also, you've gotten into a habit of hitting the ball rather than playing the game. Here's a hole where you really need a game plan. So think in terms of how you'll play the *entire* hole, not just your first shot.

The golfer hits two nice 5 woods and drops the third shot on the green about thirty feet from the pin. The putt is downhill-sidehill. It will drift to the left.

S: Those were three nice shots. Wasn't so tough, was it?

G: No, but now comes the test. I'd sure like to drop this birdie.

S: You mean you're going to go for the hole and not lag it up?

G: Why should I lag it? Listen, Doc, I may not have another chance to make a birdie here all year!

S: That's a long putt to drop, but not too difficult to get close. If you lag it, you may not drop it, but your chances of getting your par will be very good. Remember, you can't forget the odds—the *reality* of golf.

G: I can see your logic, but the birdie's too tempting. I'm going for it.

The golfer studies the putt a long time. He knows that the big danger is overrunning the hole. However, he also thinks, "Never up, never in." These conflicting thoughts create tension. He strokes the ball, but just before contact the fear of coming up short takes over. He strikes the ball too firmly. It rolls past the hole at least ten feet. Gone is his dream of a birdie. Gone, too, is much hope for a par.

S: Well, what did you learn there?

G: I learned that heroes run last in golf. I wish I'd listened to you. I had no business trying for that birdie. It was a pure ego trip.

S: Now you're catching on!

HOLES NUMBERS 5 AND 6

Golfer and psychiatrist walk up the path to the next hole. The golfer is reviewing his stupidity. He had it "made" but he "blew it." He catches himself again

*falling into the negative mental whirlpool, but he turns
it off. By thinking positively he pars the fifth hole, a
respectable 400-yarder. He feels confident as he steps
onto the tee of the sixth hole, a 330-yard par-4.
There's trouble on both sides, but a nice 200-yard drive
in the fairway leaves only an easy pitch shot to a fairly
wide green.*

*The golfer uncorks his best drive of the day, about
215 yards straight down the middle. It comes to rest
about 100 yards from the green, a pitch shot away from
a possible birdie or, at worst, a par.*

*The golfer removes his wedge from the bag and
swings confidently. What materializes is a shank. The
heel of the club line-drives the ball sharply off to the
right at about 45 degrees.*

*The psychiatrist looks carefully at the golfer, who
looks as though he's been poleaxed. There's no question
that he's in some stage of shock. The doctor knows that
he must deal with this man carefully.*

G: What happened? (*The words are barely audi-
ble. The golfer's larynx is strangled.*)

S: (*In his most dulcet tones*) Look, your game is
going great. That shot you just hit can happen to the
best. Just don't worry about it. It's an isolated incident.

*The golfer walks in silence toward his ball now
stymied behind a tree. His anger surges like a heavy
sea. He heard the shrink, but he really wasn't listening.
His inner voices are screaming too loudly: "You stupid
idiot, you had it made. Why, why, why?" There is no
answer. Just silence—and that dull throb in his head.*

S: Come on, forget it.

The shrink touches the golfer on the shoulder. This unforgivable infraction of Freudian technique shocks the golfer back into reality. The shrink repeats his advice. This time the golfer listens.

G: Well, it's pretty clear I should have gone with the 9 iron. That was an easy 9-iron shot.

S: Perhaps. Also, you were a little too cocky. You were thinking about pars and birdies rather than the problem of the shot *at hand*. You've got to play this game one stroke at a time. There's no way that you can leap over time. Your big problem now is to contain yourself. Don't let this thing throw you. You've got a good game going. All you've lost is one stroke, maybe two. But if you really let the negative garbage pour in you can scuttle your whole game. So *forget* about what you just did. Your job is to deal with the problem as it is *now*. The dream of the birdie and par are gone for this hole. Play the best golf you can to get that bogey. That is your most realistic goal.

HOLE NUMBER 7

The golfer settles down and gets his bogey. Suddenly he feels good. He's mastered his emotions. He walks to the next hole, the number one handicap hole, feeling confident. It's a 450-yard par-4. Two big hits in any man's game, but somehow it doesn't now daunt the golfer. He laces two nice wood shots, pitches on nicely with his third, and rims the cup with his ten-foot putt. He knows he's played a tough hole well.

HOLE NUMBER 8

This is a picturesque par-3 hole. The tee sits on the promontory of a hill that drops off steeply to a green 155 yards away. On the front left side of the green a small pond has a curious magnetism for golfers. Many overcompensate for it and land in bunkers on the right.

G: This hole is always a nemesis to me.

S: Doesn't seem to be that tough. What's your problem?

G: Look at that water. Doesn't that strike you as a problem?

S: That's how the architect who laid out the course would like you to think—negatively.

G: Okay, that's one of your fancy theories, but the fact is that I haven't made a par on this hole all year. On the other hand, I haven't been in the water either. I'm either long or short to the right.

S: It sounds to me like the water has you psyched out. You're not seeing a golf hole at all, just a pond. My diagnosis is that you've got a phobia about the hole mixed in with some old-fashioned masochism.

G: You told me to play within my limitations. I know I don't hit long irons well.

S: Since when is a 5 or 6 a long iron? I saw you hit a beautiful 5 iron on the first hole.

G: Yeah, but the ball wasn't setting on a tee.

S: But it should be *easier* to hit a ball from a tee —you have a preferred lie.

G: That's the problem. I can't hit a ball off a wooden tee with an iron.

S: How long have you had *that* phobia?

G: You mean I've got *two* phobias?

S: You sure have. You've got a phobia within a phobia. You're the victim of your own autohypnotism.

G: Now wait a minute! I don't mind you fitting me into some lousy Freudian diagnostic category, but that's stretching it a bit far. The *facts* are that *I can't hit with an iron off a wooden tee*, and that I don't play this hole very well. I don't see how that is related to hypnosis.

S: Actually, in your attempt to rationalize one phobia you have produced another one. Your fear of the hole is reinforced by your fear of teeing up the ball. Through self-suggestion you've involved yourself in a vicious circle of negative thinking.

G: Do you think I'll need a strait jacket?

S: Not yet. But you're sure going to subject yourself to a great deal of needless agony if you don't do something about it. You've got a little voice within your mind that keeps telling you that you're going to fail on this hole. It makes you aware of negative aspects, especially the water. It makes you forget all you've learned about the game and the swing.

G: Tell me what I've got to do.

S: What you have to do is establish a new dialogue. You know you can hit the ball 150 yards with your 5 iron. That's a *fact*. You've a right to believe it. From this elevation you aren't going to have any difficulty *reaching* the green. So, remember first to visualize the flight of your ball. Then turn your attention to your club head and bringing it squarely through the ball. Don't let yourself feel **or** think anything but success.

G: That makes sense.

The golfer sets up to the ball, swings easily. The ball comes to rest five feet from the pin.

G: I don't believe it! I've never done that before.

S: What can I say?

The golfer carefully lines up his putt and drops it for the birdie. He is ecstatic.

G: I never thought I could do it.

S: You wouldn't be a half-bad golfer if you'd give yourself a chance. But don't get carried away with the program.

G: What does that mean?

S: That means you've got a tough hole ahead of you. Don't get careless just because you made a birdie.

G: Now who's involved with negative thinking?

S: That's not negative thinking: that's *realistic* thinking. You've got to put that birdie out of your mind as much as you had to put that shank out of your mind a little while back. Keep thinking positively, but don't think that one birdie is going to make you a scratch golfer. That's what happens to a lot of guys. They'll follow a birdie with a string of double bogeys, almost as if they were punishing themselves for having dared to do something right.

G: I guess golfers are pretty sick generally, aren't they?

S: Not really. But sometimes they wander pretty close to the edges.

HOLE NUMBER 9

The ninth hole is 410 yards. Strong golfers who can drive the ball 230 yards are left with a 4 or 5 iron to the green. A knoll in the fairway that reaches its peak at about that point can produce a hilly lie, however.

G: If I can hold together on this hole, I should come in with a nice score.

S: There's no reason why you shouldn't. Just play within yourself.

G: I think I'll go with a 4 wood. If I hit it right I should have a nice uphill lie for another 4 or 5 wood going into the green.

S: Now you're thinking like a golfer.

The golfer gets off a beautiful 4-wood shot. It carries about 210 yards and finishes on an uphill lie.

S: Going with the 5 wood?

G: No, I think a good 4 wood will get me there easier. And from the uphill lie it might fly higher and a bit shorter than normal.

S: Good thinking.

The golfer hits a beautiful 4-wood shot that holds the green nicely. The ball stops about twelve feet from the pin. The golfer is once more ecstatic. This is the first time he's been on this green in two strokes all year. Again the birdie stares him full in the face.

G: I've got to think I can make it.

He lines the putt up carefully, all the time telling himself he can make it. He putts and leaves it five feet short. He can't believe it. He feels himself breaking into a sweat. He's aware of a sudden sense of deep uneasiness. The five-footer begins to look like a fifty-footer. The golfer wants to get it over with. He putts too fast,

*he ball rolls a foot past the hole, and he drops the
ap-in for his bogey.*

G: What a way to end it! But I played the hole well
except for the putting.

S: What went wrong with the putting?

G: I can't figure it out. I did everything you recom-
mended on the first putt. I really thought "positive."
What went wrong?

S: Whatever went wrong had nothing to do with
the fact that you thought positively. Thinking positively
is not going to put the ball in the hole for you. It's not
Aladdin's lamp. That's the trouble with golfers. They're
looking for the magic wand that's going to make Ben
Hogans out of everybody. Thinking positively is going
to muster everything you've got to fulfill the goal. Golf
is not magic. It deals with real-life problems. The
sooner you settle on that point, the closer you'll be to
developing an attitude that will help you become the
kind of golfer you physically can and should be.

13

Jack Nicklaus on the Couch— the Mentality of a Superstar

THERE is no special set of mental characteristics that fits all geniuses. Genius is a gift that is in many ways independent of the personality of the gifted person. In some cases the person is a genius *in spite* of his personality, rather than because of it. Even so, a look into the personality of a superstar can be helpful to many less gifted people because of what it reveals about the mental elements that produce great achievement. Genius will never be achieved solely in this way, but the inspiration and example such an examination provides can definitely contribute to higher levels of performance among lesser mortals.

There can be little doubt that Jack Nicklaus is the greatest golfer there has ever been. I don't think I could say that about any other athlete in any other sport. You could never, for example, convince me that Joe Namath was a better quarterback than Dutch Clark, or that Johnny Bench was a better catcher than Mickey Cochrane. But I really believe that Jack Nicklaus could have consistently defeated any golfer in the history of the sport. Now, I don't claim to be an expert on the inner functioning of the Nicklaus mind, but, in my brief encounters with him, several things have emerged which, if they are not the basis of his genius, must at least reinforce it in a very special way.

SELF-HONESTY

OF all the golf superstars that I have met, Nicklaus seems the least affected by his greatness. Many great achievers have a unique kind of self-consciousness that makes them appear almost aloof, which is understandable when you consider the amount of fuss that people make over them. It must become very boring for celebrities to meet so many people who just want to be able to tell others that they shook hands, etc. And there are a lot of people like this, because it's very impressive when you can tell the boys at the club that, for example, you played golf with Arnold Palmer last week. (Maybe you should also mention that you played only one hole with Arnie, at a convention where he was paid a handsome price to go one round with some of the clients. But why louse up a good story?)

I have seen Nicklaus in those situations on a number of occasions, and the most impressive thing about him is his ability to remember everyone's name. What that indicates is that, whenever he meets a person, he is able to concentrate on that person and his name with the same kind of intensity as when he zeros in on a putt. It also indicates that, at that moment of time, Nicklaus is more conscious of the other person than of what that person is thinking of him.

Somehow one always associates the genius and celebrity with social alienation: "I vant to be alone," as Greta Garbo used to put it. There is a trace of shyness in Nicklaus, but no sense at all of remoteness or aloofness. His obvious consciousness of the people he meets creates a feeling of warmth and normality—the feeling that you could entertain him as easily in your kitchen as your living room. Maybe what I'm saying is that stardom has not gone to Nicklaus's head, which takes a special kind of human quality that defies description but is a big factor in his continuing success.

His resistance to the temptation of becoming a god is definitely the chief reason why Nicklaus is less vulnerable than most superstars to being affected by the deified—and phony—stratum in which many celebrities exist. So far his extraordinary self-honesty has allowed him to live very much at the same level, in terms of self-esteem, as that at which most people live.

INHERENT HUMILITY

ALL of this leads us to what I think is maybe the true key to Nicklaus's genius, and that is his inherent humility. By that I do not mean the kind of attitude that causes some people to go around with long faces and bowed heads inviting the world to heap humiliation upon them. Nicklaus's humility is a humility of respect—for opponents, for golf courses, for the traditions and history of the game, and for people and things in general—and its greatest benefit is that it prevents him from getting carried away by his own invincibility.

The thought of invincibility is one of the biggest problems all successful people have to face. It removes the mind from the perspective of the person's own human nature, thereby opening it to all kinds of delusions. The perspective of his own humanity is something that Nicklaus has been able to hang on to throughout his twenty years of celebrity. And as long as he continues to do so, he's going to be a very, very tough man to beat in golf.

EMOTIONAL STABILITY

THE realistic perspective of his own humanity that underlies Nicklaus's emotional stability is based on his matter-of-fact attitude to the famous and glamorous people with whom his fame brings him into constant contact. There is a fascination about these people that most ordinary folk find irresistible. They seem to acquire an almost deified aura, and to be among them is heady wine for most of us. Nicklaus seems singularly untouched by such people—as untouched by the greatness of others as he is by his own.

Nicklaus's kind of humility gives birth to a confidence that is based on solid facts, on *reality*. He knows that he has to put his pants on one leg at a time like everyone else, and is therefore subject to the same problems as everyone else, one of those problems being that he isn't the same golfer day in and day out.

The difference between him and most of the rest of us is that he recognizes and accepts those differences, those variables. For example, instead of trying to crank out that extra yardage by swinging harder on those days when he is not hitting the ball flush, he accepts that less-than-100-percent performance as part of the challenge of the game. He realizes and accepts the fact that a great part of the challenge of golf (and of anything else, come to that) is not only what has to be dealt with in the external environment, but what goes on internally. Thus, on days when he's not hitting the ball so far or so straight, he is able to concentrate more on his short game, or his putting, or on some element that will enable him to "play well badly," as Bobby Locke used to put it.

What most golfers do when faced with these vicissitudes is panic, not realizing or accepting that they are inevitable expressions of the variable quality of human experience. Unlike Nicklaus, they cannot make themselves wait for the external processes to fall back into balance, which they will always do if the golfer is both patient and positive in his approach to the game. In panic, or rage, they rush off in pursuit of a new grip, or a new shoulder turn, or a new club-face angle at the top—anything but patiently sticking to the basic fundamentals.

TOTAL UNDERSTANDING

ONE reason why it is easier for Nicklaus to be patient under such circumstances is that he has a thorough *mental* grasp of every element of the game of golf. It is clear that he has searched out, with the curiosity and determination almost of a scholar, every aspect of the game that he plays so well. Thus, because he knows for sure in his mind what works best for him when he is "right," he has the patience to wait for things to fall back into balance again, while working rationally and intellectually at restoring that balance. This is yet another factor that has contributed enormously to his phenomenal success.

It is because he knows so much about every aspect of the game that Nicklaus is able to concentrate so resolutely upon what he is doing. People recognize this tremendous ability to concentrate, in conditions where most of our minds would be going a hundred ways at once, as Nicklaus's greatest single asset. A primary factor behind it is the endless working of his mind—the continual application of intellect, rather than emotion, to the job at hand. Nicklaus *controls* every move that he makes, and he makes every move to a very specific end. There are no gaps, no blanknesses, no slipping of his mind into neutral gear. The clutch of his mind responds quickly to each deliberate, intellectualized, controlled movement without pause or hitch.

Nicklaus's vast knowledge of golf derives from practical experience, not from theoretical sources, such as reading. "I've never read a golf book in my life," he told me once, with almost a fierce kind of conviction. Golf to him is a game to be learned and mastered by *playing and practicing* it, not reading about it. He doesn't criticize people who do read about the game, but he does think that many golfers go overboard in this respect. What he objects to is the implicit idea that in some page of some book or magazine the golfer is going to find the one "secret" that's going to pull it all together and keep it there. This, to him, is sheer self-delusion.

Just because Nicklaus never reads a golf book doesn't mean, of course, that other golfers shouldn't.

Jack has been playing golf since he was a child—indeed, someone once told me that movies of his swing were being made when he was only ten years old. Many people never get a chance to pick up a golf club until after they are middle-aged. Obviously such people have got to make up for a lot of lost time, and to do so they are going to have to follow routes that Nicklaus and others like him never needed to adopt.

But the real point always to be remembered is that, no matter how much you read about golf, in the final analysis you can only learn to play the game by getting out on the course and actually *practicing and playing* it. And a second point never to lose sight of—which, again, Nicklaus exemplifies—is that every person must find a method that is comfortable for himself, and then must stick to it rather than experiment with every new doctrine that comes down the pike.

TOTAL RESPECT

LIKE all top performers, Nicklaus's knowledge of all aspects of what he does has given him total respect for all the elements that go into making the whole. In golf, for example, most of us pay more attention to the long game than to any other element, for the very simple reason that this is the part of the game that propels the ball the greatest distance. Nicklaus obviously respects this aspect of the game and certainly recognizes what an advantage his power offers him. But at the same time he has total respect for all the other elements of golf. This is exemplified by the fact that, in addition to being one of the longest drivers in history, he is also one of the greatest putters—maybe *the* finest pressure putter ever.

Most golfers look upon putting as an intolerable nuisance—something that must be endured rather than enjoyed. Internally, they feel resentment that this part of the game is as important as the "more difficult" long game in terms of scoring. There is no such resentment in a man like Nicklaus. He approaches putting with the same intensity as he does any other shot—if not more so—because he realizes that a putt missed is a shot gone forever, whereas any other shot missed can be recovered from.

Indeed, among the most exciting things to watch in Nicklaus are his movements around the green. Many golfers approach the green with the sort of enthusiasm they'd have for a dull movie they'd already seen a hundred times. Nicklaus moves around the green like a starving tiger lining up a kill. And, when he's surveyed the situation, there is nothing more awesome to watch in golf than the intensity with which he goes about the act of putting. That long pause over the ball is not a grandstand play to get attention, or a sign of uncertainty, but simply *intensity* of effort. And that kind of intensity is bred only from a profound respect for what one is doing.

COURAGE

ANOTHER part of Nicklaus's make-up that is interesting to the psychiatrist is his courage. Obviously the guts you need in golf are not the same as those you need in a game like football, but golf does demand a special kind of courage. Indeed, I don't think that most people ever come close to experiencing the mental stresses that a top professional golfer goes through in tournament play, where he must continually maintain his game at its absolute peak for four straight days under constantly increasing pressure. Nicklaus, better than anyone else in professional golf at present, has the capacity to perform at peak ability when all of the forces of fear and doubt are clamoring their heads off. And that, in a word, is guts.

The same fears and doubts that beset all human beings in competitive situations beset Nicklaus—of that you can be sure. What makes him great is not lack of apprehension, but the ability to suppress apprehension to the point where his mind can focus 100 percent on his game, rather than upon himself; an ability to forget himself in a situation of stress by immersing himself in the action that causes the stress.

Most people in stress situations become so involved with themselves that their focus is forced from the action itself to what it means to them internally, emotionally. When that happens, a person invariably takes himself out of the game; becomes more concerned about his inner self than with the demands of what he is doing. The result invariably is that he loses the mental perspective that would enable him to deal with the demands of the game. When that happens failure is certain to follow. Nicklaus's ability to forget himself and focus only on the action is one of the secrets of his amazing ability to come back, even when the odds seem impossibly long, and also to stay ahead when the pressures reach boiling point—never better exemplified in his career than in the final nine holes of the 1975 Masters.

A BALANCED APPROACH TO GOLF

TO be as good as Nicklaus is at a game, you have to really love playing it. Love is what compels a man like him to put more time and effort into a single activity than others, who would like to be what he is, are willing to dedicate.

Even though Jack has this deep-seated love for this particular activity—a kind of love that is at the nucleus of the personality of all great achievers—he is not *in love* with the game of golf. A person who is *in love* with something gets tangled up with his own emotions, until the love object becomes an extension of that person himself. When that happens, what began as a love of something else ends up as an extension of self-love. And when that happens, it is impossible to sustain the degree of objectivity required to become and remain a great performer.

Nicklaus has said such seemingly heretical things as, "I love golf, but I think tennis is in many ways a better game." A person who is truly *in love* with a game could never say anything like that—it would be tantamount to self-betrayal. Because he is not consumed by the kind of infatuation that makes golf the number one priority in the lives of so many people, Nicklaus is able to maintain a balance in his approach to the game that an obsessed or infatuated golfer can never achieve. He has the emotional freedom to play and practice when he wants to, and to quit when he feels like it. There is no *compulsion* in his dedication to golf. He recognizes the importance of practice, but he does not overpractice as so many club golfers do. He can—and does—walk away from golf whenever he wants to, and I would predict that when his game begins to slip he'll walk away from tournament play just as easily as he walks into it now. In short, although he loves to play golf, he is not *compelled* to play it as a means of emotional satisfaction. Once again, that is a tremendous asset in terms of the objectivity it allows him when he runs into trouble on the course.

COMPETITIVENESS

ONE could not talk about the working of this superstar's mind without considering his formidable competitiveness. Any man who has achieved what Nicklaus has must be blessed with a truly fierce sense of competition. He must *love* personal challenge and he must *love* to win.

In Nicklaus's case, this came home very emphatically to me when I was playing with him once in Florida. The game really amounted to little more than batting the ball around and having some good conversation, and we were enjoying ourselves thoroughly in a very relaxed atmosphere. Then on one of the par-3 holes, he was called away after he had hit his tee shot. I was up next and by some strange fluke put my tee shot on the green about five feet inside of his ball.

When Nicklaus returned to the game, I had reached the green. He looked at my ball and asked, "How many are you there in, Doc?" It was a fair question, because, the way that I had been playing, the answer could have been two, or three, or six. I told him I was there in one. He looked at me very quickly, and immediately a strange transformation occurred. This relaxed, smiling, easy-going guy suddenly turned into the man you see winning Masters and Opens. He had about a fifteen-footer, and not an easy one.

Suddenly it grew very quiet. He studied the putt for a long time, wiped his putter blade against his pants, and, after that familiar long steadying of himself over the ball, stroked the putt. The ball plunked into the center of the hole as though drawn on a string. As the ball fell, Jack immediately reverted to his old relaxed self. But it was a beautiful vignette of the way the man responds to *any* competitive situation.

SENSE OF HUMOR

NICKLAUS's warm sense of humor—including a pronounced readiness to smile at himself—doesn't often come through in the charged atmosphere of tournaments. In fact, watching him in tournament play can sometimes convey the impression that ice water runs in his veins. What obscures the warmth and the humor, of course, is a competitive spirit so fierce that, under pressurized circumstances, it can totally shut out the external world. But the humor is there, and it provides a strong defense against any psychic disorders. After a poor round, his first remark to friends is almost always a light comment, generally self-deprecating. And, among close friends, he exhibits a strong sense of irony—which often, when pomposity is about, escalates to sharply pointed put-down humor. As he grows more socially confident with age and experience, this strong sense of humor surfaces more readily in public.

SINGLE-MINDEDNESS

WE have previously mentioned that Nicklaus's ability to concentrate is due largely to the fact that he has such a vast knowledge of every aspect of the game of golf, plus an ability to keep his mind working on the external action rather than on the inner self. What those qualities enable him to do is to bring his entire being to the task at hand and to shut out all distractions. *All* of the forces of his mind are directed toward what he is doing; not one extraneous thought slips through; there is nothing else in his world but the problem at hand. He could be playing with the nicest guy in the world, or with the crummiest. Such a consideration—highly important in his other life situations —has no significance to the person Nicklaus becomes in the competitive situation. His sole concern is to get that ball into that distant hole in the lowest possible number of strokes.

DISCIPLINE

DISCIPLINE is not something that you hear much about in golf, but no one better exemplifies its importance than Nicklaus. For example, he loves to eat but a few years ago decided he was too heavy. He lost a substantial amount of weight and now stays at his chosen weight through the daily exercise of considerable will power. That is a physical discipline very few people can sustain, but it is nothing to Nicklaus's lifelong mental disciplinary capacity. Even as a teen-ager, he never allowed himself to even *think* about defeat until a match or tournament was over. If any-thing, Nicklaus's self-discipline has become stronger the older he has gotten. In the 1975 Ryder Cup match his partner, Tom Weiskopf, said jokingly as Nicklaus looked over a fifteen-foot putt, "You've never missed one of those in your life, have you, Jack?" The blue eyes riveted Weiskopf as Nicklaus replied, "Not in my mind, I haven't."

Compare this response to your own behavior when you have a good score going and then suddenly slice one into the woods. Suddenly the world comes to an end. Everything is going so well, and then, like a bolt from the blue, comes a shot that makes no rhyme or reason; it simply doesn't seem fair. The anger or the self-pity begins to rise. All the starch goes out of your game, and you settle down to sullen mediocrity.

Such catastrophes happen to people like Nicklaus, and people like Nicklaus have greater reason to be angry with themselves than most of us do, because their level of skill gives them every right to expect a good shot. And people like Nicklaus *do* get annoyed with themselves over this kind of experience.

The difference between you and Jack lies in the *internal* response to the anger. Nicklaus has acquired the mental discipline to put the negative experience out of his mind and to concentrate all of his mental forces on the ball as it lies *right now*. He has the ability to bring his mind back immediately to the job at hand, rather than letting it get involved with all the extrane-ous thoughts and feelings that will quickly breed from uncontrolled anger.

This is an important part of the discipline that every

golfer must learn in order to play *consistently* well, and it applies to success as well as failure. Nicklaus is just as objective about the birdies as he is about the bogeys. Too many good shots can make a golfer susceptible to the myriad factors that can make the swing go astray by making him careless. A man like Nicklaus cannot afford ever to drop his mental guard, and neither can you if you want to play consistently up to your highest capacity.

CONSISTENT PACE

MENTAL discipline is especially important in the realm of time. There are so many situations in golf that urge the golfer to speed up the elapse of time, to jump through periods of time.

A classic situation is the tight match with only three or four holes remaining. Frequently, a certain type of golfer wishes at this point that he could pole-vault over this block of time, and it is easy to let that niggling desire eat more and more into one's game. You find yourself swinging a little faster, moving around more quickly, and suddenly the tempo of your game is lost, and with it goes the smooth rhythm that had put you in a winning position. The way in which he handles this tendency is another example of Nicklaus's superb self-discipline. He sustains the same pace through triumph and adversity, aware that time and the realities it brings must be met head-on. He is a complete master of the mental disciplines that hold the physical game together.

NO EXCUSES

HIS acceptance of reality, deriving from self-discipline and a sense of his own human vulnerability, is the reason that Nicklaus makes no excuses for his off days. Many of the lesser lights in the game will give you many excuses as to why they didn't do so well on certain days or in certain tournaments, ranging from obscure intestinal malaise to excessive amounts of humidity in the air. What these people are saying is, "I'm really great, and the only thing that prevents that greatness from being fulfilled is some problem over which I have no control."

Nicklaus never thinks that way, much less talks that way. It never occurs to him to blame anything or anyone but himself for his failures. He knows that he will have good days and bad days, like everybody else, and his honesty with himself in this respect lies at the heart of his continual efforts to improve himself.

A FRIENDLY INTERNAL DIALOGUE

NICKLAUS hates to flub a shot like everybody else, but his response is never uncontrolled rage. In fact, I believe his internal dialogue must be very kind, very encouraging, very patient—totally the opposite of the cruel, petulant, impatient, dissatisfied internal dialogue that eats away at so many of us in golf and in life generally. Anybody who abuses himself vitriolically is going to show the results in his actions. Nobody likes to be browbeaten, not even by themselves, and what begins to show up in the actions of so many people who berate themselves is the resentment that any slave feels for his taskmaster. It is my belief that Nicklaus talks to himself like a good friend. At least his game reflects that kind of dialogue.

In summary, then, we must conclude that Jack Nicklaus has a unique kind of mind that is especially suited to the game that he plays so well. Its greatest emotional strength is a rich kind of humanness that never allows him to forget his earthly perspective. Its greatest intellectual strength is an encyclopedic knowledge of the game gained through experience that began in his childhood. Deriving from these qualities is a humility that prevents his actions from being contaminated by the ego—he sees golf through the lens of reality. His love for golf is obvious, but it is not the kind of infatuation that allows the game to get out of proportion —he would not perish if he could never play again. He has an enormous capacity to concentrate. And when he's in a competitive situation, it's as though he stepped into another world that produces imperviousness to everything except the task at hand. Cementing all these assets is a special kind of courage and discipline that allows him to carry out his plans even when the odds seem irreconcilably long.

But the characteristic that stands out above all the rest is that Jack Nicklaus is a complete man, seemingly free of most of the emotional flaws that mar so many men of genius. He knows what he does have, and he knows what he doesn't have, and he can live with both. What greater qualification can there be for completeness?

14
How a Top Teacher Would Like
Your Mind To Work

I<small>T</small> was exciting riding on the top of a double-decker bus through London, looking down upon a city that I'd never seen before. My destination was the office of John Jacobs, a man who had, in years past, proven himself as a leading professional player and who now ranks as the most famous instructor in Europe. I'd met Jacobs briefly in the States and recalled him vaguely as a tall, dark-haired man who had shaken my hand and then moved on. However, the man I met in London didn't seem to resemble my image of the man I'd met in New York. He seemed younger, more handsome, than the image I had locked in my memory. An outstanding feature of the man was his brown eyes that burned with intensity as they warmed to certain subjects. When Jacobs talks to you he looks directly at you. Sometimes the messages are so clear in his looks that the words seem redundant.

From the very beginning Jacobs let it be known that he didn't entirely sympathize with what my profession had to offer golf. He said this with no suggestion of malice, his eyes smiling as if he were challenging me to change his mind. To Jacobs, golf is essentially a practical game, hewn out of man's experience with reality. No hocus-pocus, psychological or otherwise, is going to make anybody a reputable, or even a respectable, golfer.

I couldn't agree with him more. I understood his reaction to what might be called psychological gimmickry and reassured him that there was certainly no mysticism in my approach.

Jacobs's tremendous devotion to the game came across very clearly. He takes his role as a teacher extremely seriously and has that unique sense of responsibility which is part of the character of any great leader. He deplores what he calls the "diabolical themes" that have entered the doctrines of modern golf instruction, both written and spoken. He believes golf is a game made unnecessarily complicated by man. He opposes, with vehemence, the modern habit of breaking the golf swing down into a series of microscopic moves, a trend toward complication rather than simplification.

Jacobs understands the golfer who is always looking for an Aladdin's lamp that he can rub and thereby turn himself into a scratch golfer; the man who fails to realize that one of the most rewarding experiences in the game is dealing with, and overcoming, the mental and physical blocks that prevent him from realizing his full potential. Yet Jacobs does not see teachers turning students into great golfers by any magic touch. "Becoming a good golfer is something that happens inside the person himself," he points out, realizing that the ultimate responsibility for any achievement lies within the mind and body of the achiever.

The more Jacobs talked, the more I became convinced that we were saying the same things, even though we were speaking from different points of orientation. He made no bones about being an amateur in formal psychiatry—and I certainly make no bones about my lack of professionalism as a golf teacher. Yet, from what would seem to be diametrically opposite points of view, certain common denominators of thought emerged. My feeling, for instance, that golfers are too ball-oriented and not enough club-oriented, that the physical actions of the golfer affect primarily the movement of the club head and secondarily the movement of the ball, coincides with Jacobs's beliefs.

THE CRITICAL IMPACT FACTORS

IT is the simplicity of Jacobs's thinking that I found most appealing. He asked me what I thought was the most important contribution the club head made in the process of propelling the ball. I gave him a quick answer. "Club-head velocity." I'd learned that one in kindergarten. I flunked Jacobs's exam, however, because this was only one of *four* factors of impact that he feels affect the destiny of the ball. The others, in addition to club-head speed, are the direction in which the club face is facing, the path on which the club head is swinging, and the angle of its approach to the ball. In other words, the basic effects of swinging a golf club have primarily to do with what's happening to the *club head*, and not with the way one happens to place or move one's feet or head or hands.

THE FLIGHT OF THE BALL TELLS ALL

JACOBS's method of diagnosing golf problems is not related to the way a person looks when he swings a club. Rather, he forms his opinions on the basis of what the club head does to the ball. With these four primary forces in mind, one need only look at the flight of the ball to know what the club head was doing during impact. If, for instance, the ball is struck solidly but pushed to the right, I know that I brought the club face into the ball squarely and at the right incline, but the path of my club was angled off to the right. Small adjustments in stance or grip can quickly rectify such a problem. Jacobs, of course, wrote of this in great detail in his best-selling book, *Practical Golf*.

In short, what Jacobs is saying is that the point of view from which a golfer approaches the game is the most important aspect of golf. If the golfer thinks of his game in terms of "pivot," "setting the angle," "movement of the legs," "curling of the fingers," "placement of the hands," etc., he is simply putting the cart before the horse.

"What about cocking the wrists laterally?" I asked, wondering how he would feel about this basic tenet of modern golf technique.

"It doesn't work for everybody," he replied. "Ben Hogan always cocked his wrists backward. But the important point about Ben's swing is that, when the club head passed through the ball, it satisfied the four conditions affecting the distance and direction of the golf ball."

Jacobs feels that the actual muscular movement of the swing is so complicated that man could never be aware of every aspect of it. "It's a gift from above," he says, pointing to the ceiling, "that we will never really understand, but which we can nevertheless put into practical use."

Golf is not the only area in which modern man has been presumptuous enough to think that he can know all the answers. There are some aspects of human behavior that we are never going to be able to contain or control. So, in the implementation of the golf swing, man uses certain basic concepts and images, but the totality of his swing goes far beyond the understanding implicit in these fundamental principles.

A favorite working model for man's mental apparatus is that of the computer. But, as I have said elsewhere, this comparison breaks down because computers can't feel. And it's feelings that give man his biggest problems in golf. As we've explained at length, one of the biggest mental problems in the elaboration of the swing is that the golfer's mind is too susceptible to short circuits that get him emotionally involved with the ball. His major mental effort, then, must be to deal with such reflexes.

TEACHERS CAN ONLY POINT THE WAY

THEREFORE, what the teacher can give the pupil is very little compared with what the pupil can do for himself. The secret to every man's golfing success lies within himself. The teacher can only point the way, suggesting a few simple fundamentals. The student must do the job. This is the point that Jacobs emphasizes again and again.

No one can ever reach a point in his golfing experience where he feels that there's no more to learn. A great champion is not someone who has acquired an infallible method that is independent of any situation. Rather, the great golfer is one who recognizes the variations in life, and even in his own body, and is flexible enough to make the changes required to deal with the particular problems that occur on a given day. Golf is a learning experience that goes on to infinity. But the golfer must understand clearly that the solution to his golfing problems lies within himself.

Each man has a singular gift that makes him different from every other man. Jacobs doesn't feel that he can make a Jack Nicklaus out of everybody. But he hopes, by explaining the basic dynamics of the swing and the ballistics of the game, to impart to his student an attitude that will help him develop fully the potential with which he has been endowed. No teacher could ever entertain ambitions beyond that, whether the subject be golf, medicine, or anything else.

MAKING THE MOST OF WHAT YOU'VE GOT

THE use of world-wide communication today has helped make golfers more aware of other people's swings and, therefore, less aware of their own. Jacobs feels that people have the best chance of working out their swing problems by using what they've got, instead of trying to identify with one or other of the great prototypes. Today, everybody tries to swing like Jack Nicklaus or Johnny Miller, when the truth of the matter is that they almost certainly do not have the talent or experience of these men.

Jacobs seems to be saying that the secret all golfers constantly try so hard to discover by watching and emulating the moves of others may well be found instead within themselves. His creed seems to be "Play with what you've got and apply that potential to some very basic principles of the game." How could anyone fault such thinking?

OVERCONCERN WITH STARS' SWING MECHANICS

ALONG these same lines, Jacobs feels that modern instructional magazines and books are too concerned with the swing mechanics of top golfers—the men of exceptional ability who have been playing the game for years—and that average golfers trying to emulate these men are involved in impossible dreams. You can't make a silk purse out of a sow's ear, and any attempt to do so produces something incongruous— and unworkable.

Yet, many golfers spend long evenings poring over golf magazines, studying every facet of some superstar's swing in an attempt to find the magic secret. It is interesting to study the movements of any great athlete, but the information gleaned therefrom is generally of esoteric rather than practical value. If you interrogate great players, you find that they seldom read golf instructional material. This does not mean that the average golfer shouldn't read golf magazines, but Jacobs feels that he must be very careful about selecting the material he reads. The individual must learn to appropriate only the material that applies to his own capabilities.

UNREALISTIC EXPECTATIONS

JACOBS feels that some pupils try too hard. Golfing ability, like any other skill, is something that develops in its own time. The pupil who tries too hard becomes more involved with himself than with the game. The expectations of many golf students are unrealistic. They do not seem satisfied with the gradual processes of change that are so indispensable to any learning process.

Perhaps the modern demand for "instant results" in all aspects of life is one of the major deterrents in so many people's quest for the Holy Grail of golf. Another great golf teacher has said that it takes at least three years to develop a really effective golf swing. There does not seem to be any successful catalyst to accelerate this tortoise-like process.

Too often, people who desire to learn how to swing the club the right way fall by the wayside and return to their former methods because they cannot endure the humiliation and the painful metamorphosis involved in the development of a good golf swing. If a modified baseball swing can get you out there 220 yards two out of ten times, why try to change it? There may be some merit in this kind of thinking, but it all depends on what kind of a player the individual wants to be.

If a golfer wants to be the kind of player who can come through when the chips are down, then he must have a very clear understanding of the way he swings the club. It's under situations of stress that the compensations in a "Band-Aid" swing fall apart. The golfer who really understands his swing, and has grooved it physically, is free to think about the strategic aspects of the game.

FAULTY PRACTICE HABITS

JACOBS deplores the method of practicing used by so many golfers today. He says: "They go to the driving range and buy huge buckets of balls and pop them out one after another like a fat lady eating a box of chocolates."

What these golfers are hoping for is the instant manifestation of a swing that will send the ball out long and straight every time. As they swing the club, they give little consideration to what the club head is doing. It's almost as though they feel that destiny owes them a debt. If they hit 200 balls, then they feel their chances of finding the magic swing are twice as good as if they strike only 100. The mathematics is correct, but the logic is faulty. Many of these golfers find they hit, say, twenty straight balls, but the twenty-first shot strays off target. Then for about ten shots after that the balls are landing all over the park. The golfer feels a sense of panic, but he keeps whacking away, because he thinks that "the" swing will return if he keeps at it long enough.

Jacobs sees this kind of practice as a complete waste

of time. The golfer either compounds existing errors or deludes himself into thinking he has learned something when he actually has learned very little. Too often golfers have had wonderful practice sessions one day, only to find that on the course the next day they can't hit the broad side of a barn door with a scoop shovel. The magic they had in practice didn't hold together under the stressful atmosphere of a match. This puzzles many golfers and is a rich source of golf frustration.

How many times have you seen a golfer pound out straight and far a whole bucket of balls, only to flub the very last one? The problem is that, after the very last shot, you can't reach down into the bucket and pull out another ball. As Jacobs says, "The most important ball in the pail is the last one, because that's the one that's most like the true golf shot."

Practice should not be a form of exhibitionism, but a serious mental and physical workout, concentrating on those aspects of your game that are weak. Again, Jacobs's main diagnostic tool is the flight of the ball, because from this he—and the golfer himself who takes the time and trouble—can deduce which of the four possible "impact variations" have gone astray. Understanding the flight of the ball allows the golfer to make the correct adjustments to cure the obvious ailment. Without such understanding, it becomes all too easy to misinterpret the problem and, thus, to apply the wrong correction.

Golf is lucky to have a teacher like Jacobs who understands the game's physical and psychological truths so well, and who applies them so realistically. A man of his caliber could be built up into a golfing guru, with duffers from around the world coming to receive his magic touch, hoping to turn into scratch players over-night. Jacobs does have such hopefuls coming to him, but he quickly lets them know that the real problems lie within themselves. The sooner the average golfer understands the realism of learning the game, he feels, the sooner he can benefit from the help that Jacobs, and others like him, can impart.

AN OPEN MIND—AND PATIENCE

TO Jacobs, the ideal student is a person who comes to him with an open mind. It has often been said that golf is a humbling game, and it therefore follows that those who would learn to play the right way do so through a spirit of humility—not a negative form of humility, but an open mind, meaning readiness to lay aside any preconceived prejudices and to endure the long and oft-humiliating process of learning.

Ideally, a golfer must be a patient person, not looking for immediate results, realizing that sometimes it takes years to acquire the skills that will make him a respect-able player. The student must be willing for a while to see another player, who swings the club like a baseball bat, hit tee shots fifty or even one hundred yards past his drives. He must be willing to endure the humiliation of seeing his handicap go sky-high. Such a person must have faith that ultimately his work will pay off.

Jacobs feels that the old adage, "You can't teach an old dog new tricks," is a fallacy. It may be applicable to dogs, but not to man! Any man or woman can become a good golfer within the context of their own abilities if they sincerely want to. If the older person is willing to let go of timeworn prejudices, he can learn to swing a golf club as well as anyone. Naturally, he can't swing it in the same way as a young person, but then he can't do a lot of things that young people do. What he can do is swing the club to the optimum of his physical capability and then make the most of his mental equipment.

Above all, Jacobs feels that golf should be an enjoyable experience. He deplores the almost masochistic attitude of so many players. "If golf is that agonizing, why bother with it at all?" he asks. "When golf is no longer a pleasure, it's time to switch to another game."

15

Ten Questions Most Golfers
Need Answered

TRYING IMPOSSIBLE SHOTS

Q: *Why do I keep trying impossible shots—why
do I try to hit a 3 wood off a downhill lie from heavy
rough when there's no way I could even putt it out?*

A. You are influenced too much by the power
theme. You hate to use a 5 or 6 iron whenever you are
a long way from the green, because you know those
clubs yield little distance. Sacrificing yardage is offen-
sive to your Id's dream of power. You know the wood
will send the ball farther, and it seems a shame to sac-
rifice that distance just because the ball happens to be
sitting in a less-than-perfect lie. The important issue to
you is to fire that ball as far as you can. By hitting a
less powerful club, you are copping out on yourself.

In this instance, your feelings are dictating to your
intellect: in psychological terms, your Id is overriding
your Ego. Your intelligence and experience tell you that,
when you have a shot from the rough off a downhill lie,

the wood is an improper club. There is no question that, if the ball were sitting in the middle of the fairway, a well-hit wood shot would considerably outdistance a 5 or 6 iron. But it is also true that a 5 or 6 iron out of rough from a downhill lie will move the ball much farther than would a mis-hit 3 wood.

As we've said many times before in this book, you must learn to face *reality* in golf. The 3 wood is not going to function as a magic wand, suddenly altering the lie of the ball. You must learn to handle each golfing situation with the optimal equipment available to you. For example, if your ball were stymied behind a tree, you obviously would not blast a 4 wood straight toward the green, even though, if the tree were not there, a well-hit 4-wood shot would reach the green. Because the tree makes this physically impossible, you would have no alternative but to chip safely out toward the fairway.

In the situation we are discussing, however, there is no physical obstruction, such as a tree, to force your Ego to overcome your Id. Thus you choose the wood in the hope that somehow you can manipulate the club head in such a way that it will send the ball 200 yards. In short, you are hoping for a miracle. Unfortunately, they are as rare in golf as in life off the course.

FEAR OF PARTICULAR CLUBS

Q: *Why do certain clubs scare me—why am I frightened of my 8 iron when I'm perfectly comfortable with my 7 and 9 irons?*

A: This phobia indicates that at some point in the

past you had a very bad experience with your 8 iron. Maybe you shanked a shot with it in a match that had been fairly tight up until that point. The experience was so traumatic that you were shaken to the point of losing the match.

You probably told yourself that you should forget all about this catastrophe, reasoning that the more you thought about it, the more you would foul up your mind. So you tried to forget the shot and closed your conscious mind to any analysis of what caused the shank. However, your unconscious mind did *not* forget that you shanked the 8 iron, and this is what gave birth to your phobia.

An association was made in your subconscious mind that is hard to unscramble. Now, when you come to a situation that calls for an 8 iron, you subconsciously associate it with the experience of the bad shot. You take the club out of your bag, and the whole notion of disaster reoccurs, for it's the very same club with which you made the catastrophic shot.

A few practice swings may bolster your confidence, but when you stand over the ball and look down at that culprit club you are again reminded subconsciously that it was under these same sort of circumstances that disaster occurred. In your determination not to repeat that performance, you force your mind off the club head and onto the ball. Now your mind is so anxious for you to hit the ball that it leaps way ahead of the club head. The ball careens off in the wrong direction and your mind has *yet another bad shot* to associate with the 8 iron. The phobia has been reinforced, and ultimately you start leaving the 8 iron in the bag. In short, you flee from the problem; it therefore remains alive and well and stronger than ever.

This is how a phobia is created and strengthened. To get rid of it, the first thing that you have to accept is that the 8 iron itself had nothing to do with the bad shot, which was simply the result of a *single* bad swing. What you've done is hypnotize yourself into believing that the club with which you made *one* bad swing in itself had something to do with that bad swing and all the others that have followed.

To dehypnotize your mind, take your irons from 3 through 9 to the practice range. Hit the first ball with a 9 iron. Then hit balls using consecutively longer irons until you have reached the 3 iron. Notice how similar the swing is with each club. Then hit a pail of balls using different clubs at random.

Do *not* hit a pail of balls using the 8 iron only. All that would do is suggest that the 8-iron swing is somehow different. In fact, you could hit a dozen pails of balls in that fashion, and the next time you went out on the course you'd still have your phobia. Only by experimentally proving to yourself that the 8 iron is swung like all the other irons can you overcome a phobia of this kind.

DRIVER-"HAPPY" TENDENCIES

Q: *I've had some of my best rounds driving with a 3 wood but often still take a driver on all par-4 holes, even when swinging badly. Why?*

A: You are another victim of the "power" dream. You know the driver is designed to send the ball out a few extra yards, so, even though you can do well off the tee with the 3 wood, the gnawing thought in your mind is that you could do even better if you used the "big club." But that's only part of your problem.

To use the driver when you are already swinging badly is a form of masochism or self-punishment. In our thinking we often equate ineffectiveness with wrongdoing. This equating stems from past experience. For example, until not so long ago a pupil who did badly in school was punished by the teacher with a crack over the knuckles from a ruler. The theory was that the physical trauma would snap him out of his stupidity. Punishment, therefore, came to be thought of as a way to eliminate the crime of stupidity, or the sin of ineptness, as in your case of driving badly with the driver.

Now, in golfing terms your *real* wrongdoing is swinging badly. Your punishment for this is hitting a disastrous shot with the driver, which you know you can't use even when you are swinging well. You sense that the punishment of the bad shot will expiate the guilt of the bad swing by snapping you out of your stupidity. Unfortunately, it doesn't always work that way, and a golfer often falls into a glut of self-punishment that affects every aspect of his game. The end result is disaster.

Try to be objective about your game. If you're swinging badly, that's where the scoring sickness lies. Get back to the fundamentals of the swing. Are you getting too emotionally involved with the ball? Check your grip and your setup. How is the club head coming through the ball? Is it swinging *through*, or only hitting *at*, the ball?

Golf is a game to be played with the most effective equipment available to you. Don't "try out" your driver on the course if you haven't been playing with it for a long time. When things are going badly, be on guard against "magic" thinking. Golf is a *real* game, and the answers to its problems are going to be found in the realities with which it confronts you.

"NEGATIVE" HOLES

Q: *Why is it that on my home course I have one or two tees from which I nearly always drive exceptionally well, and others where I usually drive poorly?*

A: This is a common experience among golfers. There seem to be no physical factors that would account for this curious inconsistency. The same driver is used on all the tees. All the tees are flat and perfectly horizontal. What *is* different is what you see from the tee—the slope of the fairway; perhaps the way it bends; the placement of hazards, trees, or rough; and so on. But the implications of what you see are psychological rather than physical. They only become significant physically after the ball has been struck. On his "bad tees," however, the negative or threatening things he sees loom in the forefront of the golfer's mind beforehand. They become his first priority.

On the "good tees" the very opposite is true. The golfer's experience has nearly always been good, so he puts the hazards he sees into the lower echelons of his priority systems. His first priority is the designated target, and around this he orients all his thoughts and actions. He plays comfortably within his capabilities. All his thoughts are positive. It never occurs to him that his shot will be anything but good.

To know all the physical techniques in golf is not

enough. You have to be in control of your mental, as well as your physical, apparatus. The golfer has to be on the lookout for the tiniest encroachment of negative thinking, because it can destroy the finest technique in the world.

Obviously, there is no real reason why some tees should be "good" and others "bad," and it's the golfer's responsibility to make all tees "good" ones. When one of these consistently "bad" holes turns up, you should examine not only your basic physical techniques, but also the character of your thinking. Focus your mind on the *real* issues of the game.

TRANSFERRING A GOOD SWING FROM RANGE TO COURSE

Q: *Why can't I take the swing I've developed on the practice tee onto the golf course?*

A: Here you are talking about two entirely different environments, psychological as well as physical. The physical differences are important and should be recognized. On the practice tee, but not on the course, you are hitting shot after shot with the same club and with little waiting or walking between shots. It becomes easier to retain successful muscular reactions from shot to shot, much like a basketball player who stands on the free-throw line and sinks shot after shot. Also, on the practice tee you are usually playing from level terrain and preferred lies.

From the psychological point of view, if the golfer makes a bad shot on the practice tee, it doesn't affect his game, for his "game" at that particular point is simply hitting balls. There is very little pressure or stress to deal with, because the penalty for failure is minimal. He doesn't have to hit the ball particularly straight: he's looking more for solid hits or distance; he can hit as many balls as he wishes and they won't be counted against him. In fact, the popular philosophy is that the more balls he hits on the practice tee, the better golfer he will become. But the golf course is a different proposition altogether. Here, only one ball is in play, and that puts plenty of stress into this situation. The golfer knows now that each stroke counts, and if he makes too many it's downright embarrassing.

As I have stressed elsewhere in this book, most golfers don't practice to learn things that will be helpful to them on the course. To many golfers, practice is an end in itself. They believe that if they can develop a good swing on the practice tee, they can take it anywhere and use it. But often a rude awakening occurs when they take the swing that works so well on the practice tee into a competitive situation. The swing breaks down because the mind is confused by too many unfamiliar inputs.

That is why the golfer, through his imagination, must make his practice conditions as similar as possible to those that exist in the *real* game on the course. In his mind each swing that he takes on the practice tee should duplicate something that might happen in a real game situation. The golfer must never hit the ball just for the sake of hitting it. In golf, a ball is hit *to* something, and that anticipation must be a part of every practice shot. The disappointment of a bad shot, or the satisfaction of a well-placed shot, should become a part of every practice session.

It's true that the top professionals will go out and

hit a hundred practice balls after an eighteen-hole tournament round, working on some specific element of their technique. But those men are involved with problems of precision beyond the dreams of the average once-or-twice-a-week golfers. And, even though the pro may practice a great deal, there is no danger that he will ever make practice an end in itself. He knows the folly in so doing.

So the reason the swing you've developed so well on the practice tee falls apart on the golf course is that it was fashioned under noncompetitive, stress-free conditions. Use your imagination to transform the practice tee into a golf course. Don't use the same club twice in a row. Take long intervals between shots. Choose a definite target for every shot, and make it a target to hit the ball *to*, not just *over*. Conjure up in your mind familiar holes or golfing situations that are part of your actual experience. I've repeatedly warned golfers to avoid magical thinking, but what I'm describing now is not magical thinking. Rather it is the intelligent use of imagination to prepare the mind–body complex for a situation that is very real indeed.

CONSTANT EXPERIMENTING

Q: *Why can't I mentally make myself stick to one swing pattern, or putting stroke pattern, instead of constantly experimenting?*

A: Golfers are "seekers of the truth." But, like so many others, they get led down strange byways of mysticism. There is something about magic that is dear to the hearts of all men and women. We were intro-

duced to it at an early age, sitting on our mothers'
knees as we heard stories of Aladdin's Lamp, Puss and
Boots, Alice in Wonderland, and all the other wonderful fictional characters of childhood. We loved to hear
of their superhuman feats. We longed for a lamp like
Aladdin's that could produce anything we wanted. And
these fantasies of childhood still exist at certain levels
of our minds—as exemplified by the common dream of
finding money or treasure.

So the golfer in search of the perfect swing can never
be totally satisfied with what he's got. He's forever
searching for a magic wand. He tries one method but
finds it doesn't answer all of his problems in a reasonable length of time. He can't wait any longer, so he begins to wander from the basic fundamentals of the
method he has learned and steps out in search of that
one thing which, like Aladdin's lamp, can make all
his swings perfect. We live in a society that demands
instant results. We don't like to wait. Many of us don't
even like to work anymore but want things to appear
with the whirling precision of a computer whenever
we snap our fingers.

The time factor is very important in the evolution
of a golf swing. There is no way that we can rush the
swing. It unfolds according to its own sense of timing.
But there are ways of impeding its natural progress,
and one of the most effective is to confuse the mind
with a plethora of methods and gimmicks.

It is true that much of golf is "feel," especially in
putting. It's also true that this indefinable part of every
golfer's armory can't be discovered in books. It comes
only with constant practice of the *same* method. Constant experimenting with new gimmicks merely frustrates the development of feel. So decide on one method
and stick with it. Be willing to go through the "blood,

sweat, and tears" that seem to be necessary to any worthwhile learning process, and be on the alert for the voice from your infantile past that cries for the magic wand. When you identify this cry, tune it out of your system. If you don't, you will waste your time chasing golfing rainbows.

MISSING SHORT PUTTS THAT MATTER

Q: *What mental factors cause me to miss short putts on the course that I could make all day long on the practice green?*

A: The major psychological stress on the course, as opposed to the practice green, is that on the course the golfer feels he *must* make the putt. During practice there is no such compelling need. If the player misses a putt in practice, he simply puts it over again. He may have learned something from the experience, but the main thing is that he didn't *have* to make the putt.

On the course the golfer knows that sinking the short putt will help not only himself but, in many games, his partner as well. Thus the added psychological stress of responsibility and obligation bears down upon his mind. Man has difficulty dealing with responsibility, especially with imperatives like "you have to." These put him under a pressure he basically resents. The underlying thought is, "I don't *have* to do anything if I don't *want* to," but this rationalization comes apart at the seams in golf. For the player *has* to make that putt, whether he likes it or not. (It is, of course, for this reason—evasion of responsibility—that there are so many "gimmes" in club golf.)

The introduction of this pressure begins to activate

other pressures. Although he has made short putts a hundred times on the practice green, the golfer becomes aware of a fact that really didn't concern him in that nonpressurized situation—the fact that the putt could, indeed, be missed. The very act of focusing his attention on that possibility considerably lessens the chances of his making the putt. Suddenly the golfer's body begins to feel "funny." He makes a practice stroke. His putter feels awkward and unfamiliar. Perhaps he becomes aware of his heart beating at an uncomfortable rate. His hands feel clammy and inappropriately large. There seems to be something wrong with the way he is gripping the club.

He knows all this is nonsense: he's made putts like this a hundred times on the practice green. But then he begins to realize that he hasn't made *this* putt yet. Suddenly he finds himself confronting eyeball to eyeball the fact most golfers repress—that this is the only time in his life that he will have to putt in *this particular circumstance.*

He then becomes aware of time in a very uncomfortable way. He wishes he could leap over the next few seconds. As his anxiety mounts, the most important thing becomes simply to get it all over with. So he putts quickly, unthinkingly. The "ridiculously" short putt slides by the side of the cup.

Let's talk about some of the ways the golfer can deal with these psychological factors.

First, spend more time on the practice green, but putt with only one ball at a time. Don't drop three or four, because that suggests that you have three or four chances. What you have to drum into your mind is that you'll have only one chance at each shot on the course. Also, just because you're on the practice green doesn't mean that you can't imagine stress situations on each shot. You must do everything possible in your mind to simulate true competitive conditions. You'll be surprised how many stress situations you can dream up. Practicing in this way makes the transition to the real thing a lot easier, because you learn to respect each practice putt you take.

Another thing to remember is that, as we've explained at length, many golfers have a deep-seated contempt for putting. Only when a person can honestly confront that contempt and replace it with a deep-seated respect can he hope to be a good golfer. The inability to make that confrontation and conversion has brought about the downfall of many talented athletes, causing them to play a sport at a level far below their natural potential, or to give it up altogether.

COPING WITH DISASTER SHOTS

Q: *What is the proper attitude to take after you have just triple-bogeyed a hole, or three-putted from ten feet, or otherwise played disastrously?*

A: If you ever doubted the existence of a basically aggressive component in man's nature, it would be enlightening to look into the mind of a golfer who has just endured one of these golfing disasters. The cerebral scene would be one of utter chaos. Every possible force in that man's mind would be mustered for mass explosion. And, for just a few precarious moments, reason would often have actually deserted his mind. Handled poorly, that kind of rage can destroy not just a man's game but the man himself. It's an emotional experience that every golfer has to learn to contend with if his game is to survive, just as every person has to control these impulses if they are to survive.

In golf there is a reason for everything that happens, and the reason that bogeys grow into double or even triple bogeys is that the golfer tries to obliterate a mistake from his mind—as though it hadn't happened at all. Of course, "crying over spilt milk" is a waste of time and energy, but the golfer should face his mistakes with the thought of what he can learn from the experience. Once he understands how he went wrong, he can store the information in his memory bank for use in similar situations in the future.

Whatever you do, try not to get emotional about bad shots or bad luck. If you carry anger into the next shot, you're asking for more trouble. Another bad shot will mobilize even more anger, and the first thing you know you're in a psychological snowball heading fast downhill. And once the snowball has gained a certain momentum there is no stopping it until it has totally ruined your game.

So once you've learned all you can from the bad hole, discard the rest of the experience in the same way that you would get rid of garbage at the end of a meal. Focus your mind on the hole or the shot you're playing *now*, for that's the only one that counts.

In golf there are many things to remember, but the golfer also has to learn to forget. Unfortunately, human nature is such that it's easier to forget the good things than the bad. The "bad" memory has a special form of psychological adhesiveness that good memories lack. But the golfer who allows negative thinking to dominate his mind is in for a lot of suffering. He must realize that forgetting is not easy. It's a tough mental exercise that some golfers never learn. But the inability to know how to forget in golf can cause more grief than all the bad grips or bad swings ever dreamed of.

THE WANDERING MIND

Q: *In business and other things I am generally able to concentrate well on whatever I am doing. In golf my mind wanders, sometimes even while I am standing over the ball. Why?*

A: The problem of the wandering mind has plagued many golfers. We have mentioned before that the golf swing is a complicated gymnastic maneuver, much like that of diving. A diver, before he performs, very carefully goes over in his mind all of the details of that particular dive. When he has the image firmly implanted in his mind, he steps out onto the board to perform the dive. But the diver's mind does not wander, because his physical movements fulfill a very precise muscular sequence that he has already formed in his imagination. The actual move is something that he has rehearsed very carefully in his mind.

The formation of a total golf-swing image, as well as the other images that we have referred to elsewhere, must likewise be an essential part of the ritual for every golfer on every shot he makes. If the mind is not busy thinking about something, it's going to begin to wander. And thinking about hitting the ball straight is not enough. The golfer must think about the swing that's going to bring the club head squarely through the ball to make the ball go straight.

Another problem related to the wandering mind is

the time distortion in the swing. Although the actual implementation of the swing takes but a few seconds, when it is combined with the preliminaries the time elapsed can seem interminable. It's during that interval of time that the golfer can get emotionally involved with the ball and its pleas to hit it as soon as possible. The tension of waiting for the swing to unfold causes the golfer's mind to leap to the ball, or become involved with some extraneous thoughts. That's why it is so important for the golfer to focus his attention on a mental picture of the moving club head—his mind must synchronize with its movements at all times.

Before you swing, try to rid your system of tension, as I've described earlier, because if there is anything that will destroy a smooth physical or mental function, it's free-floating tension. Next, learn to think about the *movement* of the swing before you swing, in the same way the diver thinks about the components of his dive. Form a very clear mental image of what you want to do before you swing, then imitate it in physical motion. Focus your mind on that moving club head—stick right with it every inch of the way. Finally, be patient: wait for the swing to unfold itself. If you can keep your mind occupied with these things, it isn't going to wander, because it's going to be too busy.

IRRITATION

Q: *Why do I get so irritated by the habits or remarks of people I play with that I can't wait to get off the course?*

A: You're allowing yourself to become involved

with another person's game in a subjective way. This is one of the fatal errors of golf. When you find yourself being irritated by the habits or remarks of other people with whom you're playing, this is a direct warning that you are falling into a very dangerous mental hazard that can totally destroy your game. You must see this as a dangerous flaw in your *own* golfing personality.

This subjective sensitivity to the remarks and actions of other people is a reflection of your own insecurity. It's almost as if you were looking for excuses to play badly, or to otherwise feel miserable. Always remember that golf is the one game people play in which they have no legitimate right ever to blame their own poor performance on something somebody else said or did. If somebody rattles his clubs while you are addressing the ball, you really can't blame him, because it was you yourself who paid attention to the noise. If your mind was completely involved in what you were doing, it wouldn't matter if every golfer on the course began to rattle his clubs.

Getting irritated with other people's habits is just one more way for a golfer to louse up his own game. Don't go looking to other people for excuses for what's going wrong with *your* game. Golf is a game that basically involves only the golfer. His job is to get objectively involved with himself, not subjectively involved with the behavior of other people.

16

Putting It All Together
Mentally

THERE is no question but that golf is a physical game. A very lively ball is propelled with a peculiarly shaped weapon by means of a complicated gymnastic maneuver. The problems of this maneuver are increased by external factors such as wind and the density of the air. The landing of the little ball on fairway and green forces the golfer to consider beforehand the effects of friction, ground contour, turf softness or hardness, and even the blades of grass whose sharply clipped projections can determine how it rolls.

Man has given a great deal of thought to these physical aspects of golf. He has researched them exhaustively, hoping to find the secret that holds it all together. His search has been fruitful, in that he has unmasked many physical and technical mysteries of this game. But, in a sense, the more he discovers, the more complicated the problem becomes. In his quest for wisdom about the physical effects, he has always been aware that the *mind* somehow plays a vitally important part in it all. Only too often, however, men have simply acknowledged the importance of the mind, without saying very much about it. In this book we have tried to confront this problem a little more directly, daring to define the mind and the way that it operates in golf.

Although the mind is not tangible—you can't touch it or pick it up—it is nevertheless a very *real* part of man's experience. It is most important for the golfer to accept the mind as a real entity and to understand something of its inner workings. We have seen, for example, how important it is to be aware of, and to control, our emotional feelings. If we allow fear or anger to dominate our games, then we are in for a miserable experience. Certain feelings must be identified and dealt with or they will destroy our chances for success.

THINKING SUCCESS

THE golfer must always work from a hypothesis of success. If he allows doubt to leak into his mind, then his game will become an ugly caricature of what it might have been.

"Thinking success" is not self-delusional. It is an intelligent psychological attitude that is a part of every successful human experience. When you think success, everything in your body and mind is programmed to attain that goal. We can consciously control only a fraction of the muscles used in swinging a golf club. The physical move is far too complicated and quickly executed for any complete understanding of all the ramifications of the swing. It is absolutely necessary, then, that we muster our large groups of unconsciously activated muscles to cooperate in the performance of the swing. This is done through "thinking success," and by the employment of images as previously described.

THE NEED FOR HUMILITY

THE one most important mental characteristic for a golfer is humility. Learning to play golf the right way is, above all, a humbling experience, very often involving the letting go of familiar theories and sacred beliefs that have worked so well in other sports.

First, the golfer has to deal with the problem of power. We have seen how fantasies of power have become a very important part of man's emotional development, and, because the golfer has to deal with so many frustrating factors, the tendency to regress to raw power is never far below the level of his conscious behavior. If the golfer can't get the power myth squared away in his game, he will play bogey golf, or worse, the rest of his life.

To an objective observer standing on the sideline, giving up the quest for power might not seem like such a big deal. It is only when you stand straddled over the tiny ball yourself, with stick in hand, that you begin to face the struggle, and it is only after countless humiliations that you begin to get the idea that golf is really a game of *control*. Any intelligent person *should* see and acknowledge this after even only a few minutes' experience at the game. But, oh, how those intelligences shrivel up and die!

HITTING THROUGH, *NOT* AT

THEN the golfer must develop the feel of the golf *sling*. That doesn't come easily. He has to overcome all his inborn reactions to the stiffness of the shaft and the angle of the club head. But the biggest prejudice to overcome is the tendency to hit *at* the ball instead of *through* it. Hitting *through* the ball is a concept that we can hear a million times but can learn only by working it out in our own experience. How dearly we hold on to that old axiom—so appropriate in other games—of keeping our eyes on the ball! Man doesn't give up easily a belief that is so deeply lodged. But in golf we have to learn to give the club head dominance over the ball in our thinking. We must become very familiar with that club head, and its feel as we sling it. As John Jacobs has pointed out, we must incorporate into our thinking the way that the club head affects the flight of the ball. Our target image must include not only the velocity of the club head, but also its angle of approach, its path, and the direction in which it faces.

OVERCOMING BALL FIXATION

THE golfer must realize all the ways the ball can influence his mind and recognize that one of his greatest psychic battles is contending with this influence. The most important thing in a golf shot is where the ball goes, but if it is to go where the golfer plans, he must learn to almost ignore it. That may sound like a paradox, but golf is full of paradoxes.

The golfer must practice slinging the club head through a spot on the ground, to establish the "feel" of the club head as it accelerates through the impact area. When he becomes familiar with that "feel," all he must then do is introduce a ball into the path of the club head.

ACCEPTING THE FUNDAMENTALS

DURING his practice sessions, the golfer must deal meticulously with seemingly minor things, such as developing, and growing accustomed to, the grip that is best for him. Proper gripping is a physical function, but the mental problem is one of dealing with an underlying arrogance and impatience that doesn't want to bother with such mundane things. For instance, when the golfer played baseball, he didn't have to go through all this fuss. He just wrapped his hands around the handle of a bat and swung. The novice golfer doesn't realize how different the familiar baseball swing is from the golf swing he is trying to learn.

Beginners often resent the stress that professionals put on such things as setup, posture, proper shoulder and club alignment, and correct grip pressure. This resentment reflects their ignorance of the enormous ballistical problems in golf. The margin of error in ball striking is extremely small. The golfer must therefore do everything possible to diminish the probability of error. It takes only a tiny amount of tension in the hands, for instance, to destroy smoothness in the golf swing; a tiny amount of misalignment at address to activate a progression of compensations that will throw the club head out of its proper path. Many golfers don't give these problems a moment's consideration. They want to move right on to the moment of truth when the club head smashes into the ball.

What they don't understand is that the moment of truth can be realized successfully, time after time, only if they carefully plan and prepare for it. The problem, again, may seem physical, but it is born of mental laziness or ignorance. Once a golfer begins to understand and appreciate the true fundamental dimensions of his physical challenge, he can begin to acquire a humility and a respect for the game that will help him acquire a truly effective golf swing.

UNDERSTANDING WHY YOU PLAY

MOTIVATION is probably the most important drive toward the achievement of any goal, because it stimulates one to acquire knowledge and work hard to apply it. I think the golfer should really understand *why* he wants to play the game. Schiller, the great German poet and philosopher, said something to the effect that when a man stops playing a game he ceases to be a man. The same can certainly be applied to women! There is something intrinsic in almost every human being's nature that compels him or her to play some sort of competitive game. The competitive drive is a very important dimension of what makes real men and women. I think we play golf as we play any game— to round out the circle of our humanity—and that strikes me as being a very worthwhile motivation.

So one reason for playing golf is based upon the desire to make ourselves more human. There is no room on the golf course for anyone who aspires to deity. The game is too replete with experience that reflects the frailty of human life.

One of the hardest struggles for any golfer is to come to grips with his own capabilities. Golfers get into trouble when their minds begin to make unrealistic demands upon their bodies, so it is the job of every golfer to work with the material that he has and to develop it to the best of his ability. He should never fall into the destructive urge to compare himself with other golfers. Men should not play golf to prove that they are better than somebody else, but rather to keep in touch with their own individual humanity.

COPING WITH ADVERSITY

THE golfer sometimes runs into days on the course when everything seems to go wrong. He must learn to accept that these are learning days—although the hardest thing to maintain is this sort of objectivity. If the golfer gives in to subjective feelings of despair, such days become truly tragic. If he contains himself, he can learn a great deal about his game and his personal humanity.

Man generally learns through trial and error, and the more objectivity he can maintain while erring, the less frequently the errors will occur. Thus, handling bad days well is an important psychological exercise. Life itself is not always going to be a "rose garden." There are going to be days when unexpected problems occur. You can't wish them away. You must learn to play the ball as it lies. The most important working ingredient in golf—and in life—is reality. Nobody ever became a great golfer or a great person through wishful thinking.

RESISTING COMPENSATIONS

THE basic fundamental the golfer has to deal with is the swing. Watching other people swing the club gives him something with which to identify, but imitation is not enough. The proper golf swing is something that must be felt within the golfer himself. The feeling is not easily learned, because it is full of paradoxes and contradictions.

The big temptation for the would-be golfer is to compromise—to settle for less than a proper golf swing. On a lesser scale, it's the real-life battle between the crying need for immediate gratification and the long, arduous process of really learning a skill. Freud would have looked on learning golf as a conflict between the "pleasure principle" and the "reality principle," a struggle that human beings must deal with in every aspect of life. Its solution depends on what you want out of life. If you want your achievements in life to be real and lasting, you operate according to the reality principle. If you want immediate gratification, you settle for the pleasure principle.

So, a golfer who really wants to play the game the right way will learn to swing the golf club correctly. The old Broadway song, "Ya Ain't Got a Thing, If You Ain't Got That Swing," certainly applies to golf. Johnny

Revolta, one of the top teaching pros, has said that it takes at least three years for a serious student of the game to learn how a proper swing should feel. So, if you really mean business, you'll learn all you can about the swing and try to incorporate it into your feeling system without worrying over temporary setbacks along the way.

Never give up until you've mastered the proper feelings, because, once you've got them, they are yours for life. If you stop short of mastery, you'll always be chasing a good golf swing with the same futile consequences as the dog who runs after his tail.

DEVELOPING CONCENTRATION

ONE of the greatest characteristics of the master golfer is his ability to concentrate. People aren't born with this ability—they develop it. The golfer's problem doesn't seem all that profound. He must simply get the ball into a distant hole in as few strokes as possible. There are physical challenges along the way—wind, sand, water, trees, etc.—but they become major problems only when the player magnifies them in his mind. The greatest hazards the golfer must deal with are not external at all, but rather internal. Tension leaking into the golfer's nervous system can destroy his game more than all the cross bunkers or headwinds he'll ever encounter.

The more the golfer knows about the game, and about his own reactions to it, the greater will become his ability to block out negative thoughts and replace them with positive images. When Nicklaus ponders long and hard before he strikes the ball, his mind is busy reviewing the feelings and images that will cause the club head to go through the ball in a very precise configuration. Concentration in golf should lead to action, not to transcendental meditation as in Zen. And that seems to be where a lot of golfers' minds go! Good golfers don't play in a trance. They play with active minds that are aware of every aspect of the game.

Another reason for the depth of concentration of the great golfers is that they take the game very seriously. I know the natural comeback to that: "Well, he plays for big dough." My guess is that if the ordinary golfer were to play for the same amount of money, he'd still have about as much concentrating power as a flea. Nicklaus learned how to concentrate when he *wasn't* playing for money at all. He just began to take the game more seriously a lot earlier than most of us do. It's that respect for the difficulty of the game that encourages the golfer to concentrate.

STAYING OBJECTIVE

A major threat to positive concentration in golf happens to be success: the big ego muscling in and taking over the personality. The golfer who makes a birdie or two may turn away from the reality of the game, with its attendant problems, and direct his thoughts to the realm of grandeur and self-worth. He becomes uncomfortably self-conscious. Before making the subpar scores, he was a human being and accepted himself as such. He thought about success, but always with the idea in the back of his mind that something could go wrong. Success to him was a means to an end. In his transformed state, success becomes an absolute end unto itself. The successful golfer runs the risk of losing human perspective. It's as if his mind has leapt into a godlike state. Success becomes mandatory. He *expects* it. He becomes tainted with the myth of perfection. And when human beings start expecting perfection, they're in for a very rude awakening. In fact, if a human being became perfect, he would no longer be human, and golf would no longer be a game, because games are predicated on both succeeding *and* failing.

So the golfer must learn to be just as objective about his successes as about his failures. In both circumstances he must remain a human being. Success is a wonderful part of human experience, and when it comes we should enjoy it to the fullest. It should not, however, be the gateway to grandiosity. I've seen one good score throw a golfer off for a whole season.

In a certain sense, the failure that follows success is often the golfer's unconscious way of reminding himself that he's still human. It's also a form of self-punishment for treading the pathways of deity. Man may have been made in the image of God, but he is *not* God, and he knows he's not. He is sometimes capable of doing things that are superhuman, but he must never lose the perspective of his humanity.

Along with the mishandling of failure and success, another thing that can, and does, ruin the golfer's concentration is his involvement with those he plays with and against. The purpose of the game, as I have said often before in this book, is to get the ball into the hole in the lowest number of strokes. This is never done by overpowering an opponent. In fact, the role of the opponent in golf is of secondary importance, because there is really no way that he can affect your game, except psychologically. But even here the effect is not direct. His game can affect yours only if you allow it to.

What your opponent does should really be no concern of yours. Your basic game is between you and the man who designed the course. You must keep repeating this idea to yourself until you really believe it. You can't ignore your opponent and his game, but you *can* learn to observe him objectively rather than subjectively. For example, you can watch the roll of his putt and learn something from that information that will help you to negotiate your own putt. But you must not say to yourself, "I've got to make it because *he* has." An objective attitude is something the golfer must continually strive for, because without it the best swinger in the world is going to run into a lot of trouble. It's not an easy perspective to reach, but it *is* reachable.

COMPETITIVENESS

GOLFERS need a strong competitive spirit, for they are competing in the arena of a very special human experience. Although they are competing against each other, striving to win the highest prize, their real competition is against themselves. It's the universal problem of man against himself, a facet of personality every human being has to deal with. If we win this competition, then our lives and our golf games will be played with distinction.

In golf there is, of course, only one way to develop

this special competitiveness, and that is to *play* as often as you can. Golfers *play golf*—they don't merely beat balls on the driving range. It is not possible, nor is it wise, for a golfer to play competitively every day, but it is not beyond reason that a really sincere student of the game should get in two or three games a week in season. That regimen won't make you an expert, but it can keep your game respectable—and your competitive urge high.

THINKING ABOUT GOLF

WHAT you do on the days you don't play is also important. I think a golfer can make great strides toward improvement by merely *thinking* about his golf swing and his overall approach to the game. A daily thought-session, perhaps while driving to or from work, or while showering and shaving in the morning, can work wonders, because the mind then assimilates positive thoughts that it will later help you to enact on the course.

During these sessions you should concentrate on such things as how successful shots look, and how it would feel to make them happen. Visualize overcoming various golfing situations. Plan strategy for the playing of specific holes. Determine how best to handle certain shots from trouble. Remind yourself over and over that your opponent is the *course*, not your golfing companions. Think about your last round and analyze where you went wrong, and why. Make yourself aware of mental blunders that triggered the accumulation of unnecessary strokes.

RESPECTING THE OTHER HALF OF THE GAME

THE golfer's biggest psychological problems occur on the putting green. In a very real sense putting is an entirely different game. In another of those supremely paradoxical situations, the golfing battleground that separates the men from the boys is the putting green, where he-man tactics do not apply. It seems strange that this carefully clipped parcel of ground, where every lie is essentially the same, where the same kind of club is used by each and every player, where all of the muscles in the world won't get you to first base, where little old ladies in white ankle socks can succeed just as effectively as the ripply-muscled lad straight out of college . . . it seems strange that this is the stage where the strong and mighty so often fall.

Any golfer who ever amounted to anything in big-league competition could putt well. The graveyards of the "also rans" are crammed with headstones inscribed with epitaphs reading "Big hit, no putt." There seems to be something almost inhuman about the lack of distinction between the putt and the other shots. Why should a maneuver that propels a ball only 10 feet have the same importance, scorewise, as an action that propels the ball 250 yards? It just doesn't seem *fair*. But, alas, as every golfer knows when he totals his strokes, there is no distinction made between the two. The most important thing is not what *kind* of strokes you made, but how *many* you made. This curious equality of things that are physically unequal is another vexing aspect of the game that has to be accepted and respected.

It is therefore one of the major tasks of anyone who

really wants to play the game well to convince himself that putting is just as important as any other part of the game. If he can convince himself of this, he will give putting as much time and thought as he devotes to the rest of the game.

There are limits to what someone can learn from another about putting. The swing is so simple that a person with a minimum amount of athletic ability could learn it in less than an hour. But it's not the swing that's so important in putting: it's the "touch" or "feel." You can't learn "feel" from reading a book or receiving instruction. It can come only from within yourself. To get that magic touch, you've got to be willing to spend a lot of hours on the putting green, trying to acquire a precision much greater than that required in most sports. The amount of precision you can develop is limitless. Any good putter can get better through practice. And the more one practices, the more he also develops the knack of determining correctly just how terrain and texture of the green will affect a given putt.

Many golfers can't be bothered to make this change of emphasis in favor of putting as opposed to the other shot-making areas. Their systems are programmed for macroscopic, not microscopic, problems. But unless the golfer achieves this transition, he's left with only half a game. Without attitudes of respect and humility, the golfer can never even begin to learn a part of the game that is probably the most exciting of all, in that it is the final determinant of the *score*, by which all of us are judged.

So golf is a game that employs the mind in very special ways. The golfer doesn't have to think quickly, like the tennis player whose ball is moving at high speed. The golfer's ball doesn't move at all until he hits it. The mind in golf is used in a more deliberate and calculating way. The golfer very carefully lays plans and then tries to fulfill them. His deliberation involves judgment regarding which club to use and how to use it. He must be able to deal with success and failure. He must know when to be heroic and when to be cautious. He must strive for objectivity in his game and must guard against subjective involvement with another player's game. He must gear all his actions to success but must know how to accept defeat.

The golfer must not only be able to deal with the vicissitudes of weather and the fate of the ball on the course, but also with the variations that occur in his own mind and body from day to day, and even from shot to shot. He must be always a student. He must never get to a point where he thinks he knows all there is to know about the game. When he begins to feel that way, new problems arise to confirm that the enigma of golf will never be completely solved.

The same thing can be said about life. The two processes are so very alike that one has to be a microcosm of the other. And, if you're a real golfer, it's not difficult to decide which is the "microcosm" and which is the "other"!

David C. Morley

DAVID CLARK MORLEY was born in Philadelphia and educated in the United States until the age of twelve. The family then moved to Canada. In 1942 he entered the United States Naval Air Corps as an aviation cadet. On completion of training he received his navy wings and was sent to the South Pacific as a pilot.

After the war he returned to Canada and entered college. In 1956 he graduated in medicine from Queens University. This was followed by post graduate work in psychiatry at New York Hospital and Cornell Medical Center.

He married Marion Greenhow Morley in 1944 and has four children—David, Rick, Mark and Leslea. He lives and practices private psychiatry in Greenwich, Connecticut, and is attending physician on the staff of Greenwich Hospital and psychiatric consultant at the McAuley Mission in New York City. He authored a regular column in *Golf Digest* from 1971 through 1974.